LITERACY CENTRE
Teacher's Resources

purple /blue

Poetry

Elspeth Graham and Mal Peet

CREDITS

Published by Scholastic Ltd,
Villiers House,
Clarendon Avenue,
Leamington Spa,
Warwickshire CV32 5PR

Printed by Bell & Bain Ltd, Glasgow

© 2002 Scholastic Ltd
Text © Elspeth Graham
and Mal Peet 2002
1 2 3 4 5 6 7 8 9 0   2 3 4 5 6 7 8 9 0 1

SERIES EDITOR
Huw Thomas

SCOTTISH CONSULTANT
Sue Ellis (page 8)

AUTHORS
Elspeth Graham and Mal Peet

EDITOR
Clare Gallaher

ASSISTANT EDITOR
Dulcie Booth

SERIES DESIGNER
Joy Monkhouse

DESIGNER
Mark Udall

ILLUSTRATIONS
Ray and Corinne Burrows (pages 15, 17,
30–1, 33, 114, 120–1, 123, 125)
Forepoint (pages 82–7, 89, 90, 94)
Paul Howard (scans from *The Walker
Book of Classic Poetry and Poets* pages
18, 32, 36, 44)
Valerie Littlewood (pages 55–6, 59, 62,
68–9)
Nick Maland (scan from *The Forsaken
Merman: The Wayland Book of Story
Poems* page 111)
Tony Ross (scan from *Balloon Lagoon
and the magic islands of poetry* page 66)
Mark Udall (pages 58, 61, 83, 115)

British Library Cataloguing-in-Publication Data
A catalogue record for this book is available from the British Library.

ISBN 0-439-01993-1

ACKNOWLEDGEMENTS

The Publishers wish to thank:

Amazon.com, Inc for the use of the screenshot and review of *Classic Poetry: An Illustrated Collection* which appeared on www.amazon.com © Amazon.com, Inc, all rights reserved. *The Argotist* on behalf of Ian Burns for the use of two extracts from an interview of Benjamin Zephaniah by Ian Burns in the first issue of *The Argotist* © *The Argotist*. **Egmont Books Ltd** for the use of 'Spell to Banish a Pimple' from *Life Doesn't Frighten Me At All* by John Agard © 1989, John Agard (1989, William Heinemann). **Forepoint (previously known as The Point Communication)** for the use of artwork from *Talking Turkeys* by Benjamin Zephaniah © 1995, Forepoint (1995, Puffin). **David Higham Associates** for the use of 'Dream Variations' and 'Mother and Son' by Langston Hughes from *Collected Poems* by Langston Hughes © 1995, The Estate of Langston Hughes (1995, Knopf). **Hodder & Stoughton Publishers** for the use of one illustration from *The Forsaken Merman: The Wayland Book of Story Poems* selected by Berlie Doherty, illustration © 1998, Nick Maland (1998, Hodder Children's Books). **John Murray (Publishers) Ltd** for the use of an extract by John Betjeman © John Betjeman. **The Peters Fraser and Dunlop Group Ltd** for the use of an extract from 'A good poem' by Roger McGough which appeared in the postscript by Sir John Betjeman to *The Dragon Book of Verse*, edited by Michael Harrison and Christopher Stuart-Clark © 1997, Roger McGough (1997, Oxford University Press); 'Secrets 1–13' from *The Thirteen Secrets of Poetry* by Adrian Mitchell © 1993, Adrian Mitchell (1993, Simon and Schuster Young Books); 'My Last Nature Walk' and the poem's glossary from *Balloon Lagoon and the magic islands of poetry* by Adrian Mitchell © 1997, Adrian Mitchell (1997, Orchard Books); an extract from 'The Wildest Wheelbarrow' from *The Thirteen Secrets of Poetry* by Adrian Mitchell © 1993, Adrian Mitchell (1993, Simon and Schuster Young Books). *Educational Health Warning: Adrian Mitchell asks that none of his poems are used in connection with any examination whatsoever.* **Tony Ross** for permission to reuse an illustration from *Balloon Lagoon and the magic islands of poetry* by Adrian Mitchell, illustration © 1997, Tony Ross (1997, Orchard Books). **The Society of Authors as the representatives for The Literary Trustees of Walter de la Mare** for two uses of 'Silver' by Walter de la Mare from *The Complete Poems of Walter de la Mare* © 1969, Walter de la Mare (1969, Faber & Faber). **Walker Books Ltd** for the use of illustrations, scanned into black and white, from *The Walker Book of Classic Poetry and Poets* selected by Michael Rosen, illustrations © 1998, Paul Howard (1998, Walker Books). **AP Watt Ltd on behalf of Michael B Yeats** for the use of an excerpt from 'The Lake Isle of Innisfree' by WB Yeats © WB Yeats. **Young Writer** for the use of two extracts from an interview with Benjamin Zephaniah © Young Writer www.youngwriter.org (tel: 01544 318901). **Benjamin Zephaniah** for the use of an extract from the website www.oneworld.org/zephaniah/oral_poetry.html © 1995, Benjamin Zephaniah (www.benjaminzephaniah.com).

CONTENTS

INTRODUCTION   5

Quick guide to texts and levels   9

CORE BOOK

The Walker Book of Classic Poetry and Poets   10

Shared text activities   11

Shared texts   15

Guided reading notes   19

Activity notes   22

Photocopiables   29

Extra text

Extra text notes   37

Extra text: Amazon.com® book review   39

Extra text photocopiables   40

Assessment

Assessment notes   38

Assessment photocopiables   43

GUIDED BOOK EQUIVALENT LEVEL TO CORE BOOK

The Thirteen Secrets of Poetry   45

Guided reading notes   46

Activity notes   49

Photocopiables   55

Extra text

Extra text notes   64

Extra text: My Last Nature Walk   66

Extra text photocopiables   67

Assessment

Assessment notes   65

Assessment photocopiables   70

CONTENTS

GUIDED BOOK FOR LESS CONFIDENT READERS

Talking Turkeys — 72
Guided reading notes — 73
Activity notes — 76
Photocopiables — 82

Extra text
Extra text notes — 91
Extra text: Interviewing Benjamin Zephaniah — 93
Extra text photocopiables — 94

Assessment
Assessment notes — 92
Assessment photocopiables — 97

GUIDED BOOK FOR MORE CONFIDENT READERS

The Forsaken Merman: The Wayland Book of Story Poems — 99
Guided reading notes — 100
Activity notes — 103
Photocopiables — 110

Extra text
Extra text notes — 118
Extra text: Shocks, scandals and gruesome murders — 120
Extra text photocopiables — 121

Assessment
Assessment notes — 119
Assessment photocopiables — 124

SUPPLEMENTARY BOOKS

Hello New! — 126
Collected Poems for Children — 127
Meeting Midnight — 128

# INTRODUCTION

Scholastic Literacy Centres are ready-made collections of quality children's literature put together by teachers for teachers. This resource helps teachers by:
■ selecting tried-and-tested children's books, each title chosen because it not only appeals to young readers but also draws out responses from them
■ supplying activities and information that help them to make the most of children's reading.

The teaching approach

This teacher's book has been structured to offer maximum flexibility for the various ways of working with books in today's classroom. It suggests:
■ ways to work with the whole class in shared reading
■ ways for setting up independent group work.

The approach makes books accessible to less confident readers through whole-class shared sessions, while allowing the more confident to read widely and respond at a deeper level to the books they read. The guided reading notes show teachers how to work through a book with a group of readers. The independent photocopiable pages, with their interactive style, foster reading independence in young readers and motivate them to read more widely.

The teacher's book gives opportunities for writing which build on reading, whether as a model for writing, or as a stimulus. It also suggests ways of linking reading and writing, building on teachers' experience and confidence in teaching reading, and extending these to teaching writing.

The photocopiable activities provide ample opportunities and forums for speaking and listening, whether in group discussion or in drama and role-play activities.

Selection of children's books

The children's books in each Literacy Centre resource a particular genre of fiction, non-fiction or poetry. Furthermore, they make particular reading demands on children, appropriate to the target age of each Centre. In these ways, the resource enables the books children read to work harder for teachers, allowing them to maximise the literacy and response potential of each one. Because each Centre is put together for a particular age group, progression is achieved from set to set. In addition, as the book selection in each Centre encompasses a range of reading abilities, progression is ensured within any particular set.

The core book and shared reading

Each Centre has a **core book** to be used with the whole class, either as a shared text or as a class reading book. It is chosen because:
■ it fits the range for the Centre
■ it will capture the imagination of children in the class
■ it can be used for whole-class teaching in a mixed-ability class

■ all children will be able to access the spirit of the book as well as mechanically decode it

■ it can be used to deliver the appropriate text-level literacy teaching objectives for the age group.

Three guided books

Each Centre has three **guided books** to be used for guided group reading. Like the core book, these books are chosen so that:

■ they fit the range for the Centre

■ they can be used to deliver the appropriate text-level literacy teaching objectives for the age group.

The three guided books plan for a range of abilities within a mixed-ability class and are selected for their differing reading demands:

■ one book is roughly equivalent to the reading level of the core book

■ one book is suitable for less confident readers

■ one book is suitable for more confident readers.

Teacher's resource book

In this resource book you will find four separate chapters of information and activities, corresponding to the four different children's books in the Centre. Each chapter contains:

■ information about the book, for example author notes, how it connects with sequels, background to the writing

■ guided reading notes indicating how the text can be read and re-read or split up over time – these may include questions that arise from the text, discussion points that emerge during reading, issues that focus the reader's attention, connections that can be made, and things that the children should look out for as they read the book

■ guided reading activities based on the book, plus linked photocopiables – these interactive activities, which further engage children in the book, are designed for independent group work; they keep children focused on the text and could include times when the guided reading groups split into pairs, make notes or do some guided writing

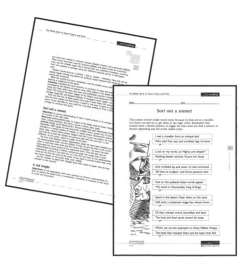

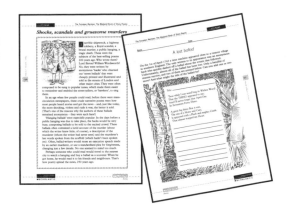

■ an extra photocopiable text, chosen because it links with and supports the book, for example a poem, a newspaper story or simply a montage of pictures – this has accompanying teacher's notes and three photocopiable activity sheets

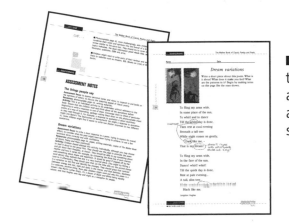

■ two assessment photocopiables, with teacher's notes, each providing an activity to check children's knowledge of and response to the book; one of these should be done without access to the text.

The core book chapter

In addition to the above, the core book chapter has a shared reading section. The four shared texts (pages 15–18) give as many children as possible access to the core book through whole-class shared reading sessions. Drawn from the core book, the shared texts may include extracts, quotes, illustrations, selections of lines or dialogue. The shared texts are designed for photocopying onto A4 for individuals or pairs to read, or onto OHTs. They can also be enlarged to A3 for display.

Teachers should use the shared texts in the context of reading the book. How the teacher achieves this depends on the particular class: it may be that the teacher reads parts of the book to the class, or with a guided group or groups, or sets children to read independently in groups, in pairs or as individuals.

Each shared text has one page of shared text activities (pages 11–14). These suggest things for the teacher to point out and discuss with the children during a whole-class session.

Supplementary books

At the back of the book (pages 126–8) is a section of activity ideas for three supplementary books. Though not supplied as part of the Centre, the supplementary books link to the Centre's text range and teaching objectives, and are given here as suggestions for further widening the range of children's reading. One of the supplementary books suggested is intended to provide a particular reading challenge for the age group using the Centre.

Using Scholastic Literacy Centres in Scottish schools

The Scholastic Literacy Centres have been written to help schools build on the high standards for literacy that are being achieved in P1 and P2. They will be especially welcomed by schools and teachers who are looking for materials to develop a broad and robust programme for teaching and promoting literacy from P3 onwards. As part of such a programme, the Scholastic Literacy Centres can help raise standards by:

■ ensuring progression and breadth in the reading material
■ encouraging teachers to use the full range of classroom organisations and teaching techniques, selecting that which is most appropriate for the desired learning outcome
■ ensuring that the reading–writing links are explicit so that children begin to use their experience as readers to inform their writing and to use their experience as writers to make them efficient and effective readers
■ addressing the gender gap in reading by specifically targeting titles and activities which are exciting for both boys and girls
■ introducing children (and teachers) to new authors and books, encouraging children to read a wider range of fiction and non-fiction for pleasure.

Teaching beyond the earliest stages of literacy

Schools which achieve high standards in literacy have teachers who:

■ have high expectations and teach for success
■ give literacy a high profile, ensuring that it is visible and part of the social currency in school
■ are clear about the specific knowledge and skills children need to learn and have a good range of strategies for teaching them
■ recognise the value of differentiation and group teaching but also use whole-class teaching and individual tasks effectively to achieve specific outcomes.

Scholastic Literacy Centres have been designed to promote such teaching. They offer a flexible, progressive framework for teaching literacy which fits perfectly with the approaches used in Scottish schools. The activities target all the Reading strands in the 5–14 Language Guidelines: 'Awareness of genre', 'Reading for information', 'Knowledge about language', 'Reading to reflect on the writer's ideas and craft', 'Reading aloud' and, of course, 'Reading for enjoyment'. The use of the texts as models and stimuli for writing allows teachers to cover key elements of teaching for the Writing strands 'Functional writing' and 'Imaginative writing'.

Organisation and teaching in the classroom

The quality of the texts and activities chosen for Scholastic Literacy Centres as well as the way in which it encourages good use of the teacher's time gives the very best support for developing a programme of work to help children become confident, fluent readers.

The **core book** provides a common literacy experience for the whole class. This ensures that children of all abilities learn to share and discuss key literacy issues and enables the teacher to both model and teach key ideas. Whole-class work, using the shared texts, develops the children's awareness of the different genres, promotes comprehension skills and highlights the craft of the writer as well as ensuring that the children are introduced to a broad range of fiction, poetry and information books.

The **guided books** can be used with ability groups to further develop these points. The children read texts closely matched to their reading abilities. They practise reading skills and learn to recognise and adopt appropriate reading behaviours for the different text organisations and purposes.

Finally, the **supplementary texts** guide teachers by suggesting books to further extend and develop particular interests and skills, helping to develop a rich and supportive literacy environment in the classroom.

QUICK GUIDE TO TEXTS AND LEVELS

Scholastic Literacy Centre Purple/Blue:
Poetry

Section	Pages	Title	Approximate level of activities
Core book	10–36	*The Walker Book of Classic Poetry and Poets* selected by Michael Rosen, illustrated by Paul Howard	Level 4 Scottish Level C–D
Extra text for core book	37–42	Amazon.com® book review	Level 4 Scottish Level C–D
Guided book (equivalent level to core book)	45–63	*The Thirteen Secrets of Poetry* by Adrian Mitchell and Valerie Littlewood	Level 4 Scottish Level C D
Extra text for guided book (equivalent level to core book)	64–9	'My Last Nature Walk' by Adrian Mitchell	Level 4 Scottish Level C–D
Guided book (less confident readers)	72–90	*Talking Turkeys* by Benjamin Zephaniah	Level 3–4 Scottish Level C–D
Extra text for guided book (less confident readers)	91–6	Interviewing Benjamin Zephaniah	Level 3–4 Scottish Level C–D
Guided book (more confident readers)	99–117	*The Forsaken Merman: The Wayland Book of Story Poems* selected by Berlie Doherty	Level 4–5 Scottish Level C–D
Extra text for guided book (more confident readers)	118–23	Shocks, scandals and gruesome murders	Level 5 Scottish Level D
Supplementary books (more challenging)	126–8	*Hello New!* edited by John Agard *Collected Poems for Children* by Gareth Owen *Meeting Midnight* by Carol Ann Duffy	

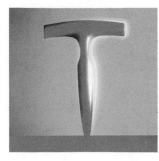

HE WALKER BOOK OF CLASSIC POETRY AND POETS
SELECTED BY MICHAEL ROSEN
ILLUSTRATED BY PAUL HOWARD

About the core book

The most immediately striking thing about this anthology is that it is a rather beautiful object. It looks and feels elegant and sumptuous. The contents pages, with their 'tiled' portraits, are far more inviting than the usual plain list. But these illustrations – and the short biographical notes which accompany them in the main body of the text – are not there merely to prettify. In his introduction, Michael Rosen points out that this is a book of *poets*, as well as poems, and that each of these men and women was an individual with his or her unique experience and vision – and face.

Classic is a troubling word. Rosen defines it in a conventional way: classic poetry is poetry which has *lasted*, remained popular and significant, for a long time – which implies that something classic must be relatively old. However, children will have heard the word used in other ways: to describe a recent album or book (an *instant classic*), a haircut, a cup-winning goal, or just generally as a term of praise. The word has become entangled with *good* and *great*. And thus a problem arises: children might feel inhibited when it comes to expressing their own feelings and judgements about a poem included in a posh volume with *classic* in the title; they may feel constrained by respect. But the poems in this collection are not equally good; it is worth remembering that clumsy poems can become 'classic' if they somehow touch a chord within us.

Teachers will have their own strategies for working with anthologies; this collection seems to invite a chronological approach, but with such a wealth of material cherry-picking will be unavoidable. We have chosen to write shared reading notes on four poems which seem, to us, to span a range of forms and styles. We are not suggesting that these particular poems are in some way 'better' than others.

About the compiler

Michael Rosen is a name which may be well known to children, since he is a prolific and successful writer. His *We're Going on a Bear Hunt* will be familiar to most schoolchildren, and there are few anthologies of children's poetry in which he doesn't appear. Interestingly, his own poetry is very unlike the poetry in this anthology. He usually writes in a very free, colloquial style about vividly recalled childhood experiences. (There's an example, 'Mart', in *The Forsaken Merman: The Wayland Book of Story Poems* in this Literacy Centre.)

About the illustrator

Paul Howard is prominent in the Walker 'stable' of illustrators – children might well know *Rosie's Fishing Trip* or *A Year in the City*. What's impressive about his work in this book is its versatility; while the illustrations all bear the stamp of his individual technique, they vary enormously according to the mood of the particular text. It is hard to believe that the cartoonish brashness of his drawings for 'Mulga Bill's Bicycle' (pages 107–9) is from the same artist who created the blue moodiness of the illustration to Frost's 'Stopping by Woods on a Snowy Evening' (pages 130–1).

Jacques

Background

Although this text works beautifully as a poem, it is in fact a speech – a monologue – from Shakespeare's play, *As You Like It*, written in (probably) 1599 and perhaps first performed in Shakespeare's brand new Globe theatre. As such, it tells us a good deal about the character who speaks it. Jacques (pronounced here as 'Jack-wez' or perhaps 'Jakes') is witty, opinionated and rather pretentious – he likes slipping French words into his conversation. He is (or pretends to be) also melancholic and cynical; life, he says here, is a black joke – we perform all these ludicrous roles only to end up helpless as babies again. And then we die.

The extended metaphor here is interesting, though; if we are all merely players, who writes the script? Who directs?

Formally, this is blank (that is, non-rhyming) verse. Its structure depends upon patterns of repetition and an underlying rhythm – five 'beats', or stressed syllables, in almost every line.

■ Read aloud the biographical note on page 12 of the book, then read the poem on an enlarged copy of photocopiable page 15. Approximately how long ago do the children think the poem was written? What do we call that historical period? Who was England's ruler? Can the children remember details, famous people, events from that time? Even without the biographical note, how can we tell the poem was written a long time ago? Encourage the children to guess or deduce the meanings of these words: *mewling* (whining), *pard* (leopard), *jealous* (fiercely protective – of his own honour), *capon* (chicken), *saws* (old sayings), *modern instances* (recent examples of legal decisions), *pantaloon* (a clownish old man, a fool), *sans* (French for 'without').

■ When the children have a grasp of these meanings, remind them that this speech is from a play. How might an actor read these lines? What expressions and body language would be appropriate? Read the poem again with as much spirit as you can muster.

■ Look closely at each of Jacques' seven ages: what do we notice about the way he describes them? It's all very *negative*. Children are *puking*, then unwilling; the lover is plain daft, composing ballads to his girlfriend's eyebrow (!); the soldier's reputation is just a *bubble* (not the safest item to find in the muzzle of a cannon); the magistrate is fat and pompous. And then it gets worse. Can the children suggest stages of a man's life that Jacques misses out – ones that might be about *happiness* (for example, getting married, becoming a father)? What does all this tell us about Jacques? What words can the children suggest to describe his personality? Why does he begin with *exits* (ends, or deaths) rather than *entrances* (beginnings, or births)?

■ This speech is based on the idea that one thing (human life) is somehow like another (acting parts on the stage). What is the word for this 'trick' in writing? (*Metaphor*.) Is it a good metaphor? It suggests that we all 'act out' our lives as if we have no choice in the roles we play; do the children think that's true? It also suggests that life is merely a play; what is funny (ironic) about a character in a play saying that?

■ What do the children notice about the way this speech, or poem, is written? Do the lines rhyme? Does each 'act' of life begin on a new line? (No: Shakespeare needed this to sound like someone actually talking, rather than reciting.)

The Destruction of Sennacherib

Background

What rises from the page is Byron's slightly suspect excitement as he expands upon and relishes this incident from the Old Testament. Byron was not conventionally religious; what inspires this poem is not faith, but a sort of gleeful, horrified thrill at imagining the event itself. It is a rather lurid, sensationalist piece, but it has a terrific energy to it. Similes of natural forces (attacking wolves, wind-blown leaves, a stormy sea) are stitched together by strong, simple, insistent rhymes and a relentless, charging rhythm.

■ Read the biographical note on page 27 of the book. They might like to know that Byron was a great celebrity, like a rock or movie star today. Many people found his behaviour scandalous; others hero-worshipped him.

■ Read the poem (with just a touch of melodrama) on an enlarged copy of photocopiable page 16. Ask the children if they can summarise the story, then read with them Rosen's explanatory note on page 154; how close did they get?

■ The *sound* of the poem is really important. What can the children say about the rhymes and the pattern they make? The lines seem at least as long as Shakespeare's, but they have only four beats instead of five; and the stressed syllables are usually preceded by two unstressed ones:

*Like the **leaves** of the **for** est when **Sum** mer is **green**.*
de de **dum**   de de **dum** de de **dum** de de **dum**

Read stanza 3 again, giving plenty of emphasis to the stressed syllables. In this stanza, Byron uses a well-known trick to give extra punch to the rhythm of the second and fourth lines – ask the children what it is. (Alliteration: *face/foe, hearts/heaved.*)

■ In the third stanza, and throughout the poem, Byron uses another repetition trick to make the poem almost a chant, a spell or incantation to conjure up the picture in the reader's mind. Can the children spot it? (The word *And* begins most of the lines, which also gives an impression of the poem excitedly and breathlessly rushing on to the next event or detail.)

■ In the fourth and fifth stanzas, Byron's imagination tracks, like a movie camera, across the scene, the thousands of corpses, focusing on details here and there: a horse's nostril, the dew on a soldier's brow, silent tents. Can the children imagine these lines as one of those long, slow tracking shots in a movie? Would such a film sequence have a soundtrack of stirring music? Or dead silence? What do the children think of the illustration on pages 28–9?

■ In the last line of the poem, the first beat comes in earlier: *de-**dum**, de-de-**dum**, de-de-**dum**, de-de-**dum**.* Can the children suggest why? (The slight change gives the final climactic line a bit of extra 'punch'.) And isn't that simile terrific? It makes us imagine God's eyes giving out great beams of hot light, so that even a *glance* is enough to melt ice.

Silver

13

SCHOLASTIC LITERACY CENTRES

Background

Walter de la Mare wrote his poems in the first half of the 20th century, but there is something about his style and use of language which seems to come from an earlier time; there's not much difference in 'feel' between this and Wordsworth's 'The Sun Has Long Been Set' (page 23). This is partly because Walter de la Mare liked old words (archaisms) such as, in this poem, *shoon* for *shoes*; but the more important reason is that his poems are filled with a yearning for an earlier, more 'innocent' or 'Romantic' time. However, it would be a mistake to see his poems as 'slushy'. This poem works because it is built on a truly rigorous and muscular structure. It's a fascinating mixture of dream and skilful technique.

■ Read the poem, using an enlarged copy of photocopiable page 17. Try to take the poem quite slowly (the first two words cue the way to read it) without crossing the boredom threshold.

■ If the group has studied Byron's 'The Destruction of Sennacherib', you may have discussed the way the poet's imagination 'tracked' like a movie camera; can the children see the same sort of thing here? Whose 'eye' are we looking through in this poem? We are asked to see (peer at) what the moon *sees* as it travels across the sky – a bit like a videocam with a spotlight attachment, plucking details from the darkness as it moves. So how is the moon imagined here? (As a person – someone walking through a landscape, lighting it up as she passes.) Do the children know what we call this writing technique, when non-human things are described as if they were people? (It is a form of metaphor called personification. Here, the moon is a woman who *walks* and *peers* and wears shoes.)

■ Does the poem 'tell a story'? (No, and if you have read the previous shared reading poems by Shakespeare and Byron you could ask the class to contrast them with this poem, which is purely descriptive.) What words might describe the scene? *Calm, tranquil, quiet, peaceful, safe*? But is this a *real* world? Was anywhere truly as peaceful as this – even the English countryside a century ago? Is the poet describing something real – or a dream, a fantasy, of peacefulness?

■ Look closely at the form of the poem. How many full stops are there? (There is just one, at the end.) This is all one sentence; like the moon travelling across the sky, the poem doesn't halt. There is the same number of beats (four) per line as in the Byron poem – **Slow** *ly,* **si** *lent ly,* **now** *the* **moon** – but this one moves much more slowly and unexcitedly. One reason for this is the great number of soft, slow sounds in the poem; can the children spot all the *s, sl, sh, st* sounds, and all the long *ee* and *ea* vowels? And can they see how lots of punctuation slows down the way we read?

■ As well as rhyme and rhythm, Walter de la Mare uses other patterns to give the poem a strong shape. What is the key word? Can the children spot that the word *silver* (and *silvery* in one case) occurs only in alternate lines? Can they see that almost every line has alliteration or internal rhyme? So although this might seem, at first, like a dreamy or even sentimental poem, it has a very strong internal organisation; it's technically a very skilful piece of work.

Mother to Son

Background

Alert readers will have noticed that in this collection it's the Americans who are more experimental with form: Whitman and Dickinson, Eliot and Sandburg. This is a free verse poem in vernacular language by Langston Hughes. It was Eliot and his fellow American Ezra Pound who pioneered free verse – verse 'freed' from conventional devices such as regular patterns of rhythm and rhyming stanzas. The essential idea behind free verse is that the poet evolves a form which best suits his subject and voice, rather than using one 'off the peg'.

Impoverished Harlem seems a long way from the fantasy forest in which Jacques languished in *As You Like It*. Interestingly, though, Hughes and Shakespeare are doing something similar: exploring an extended metaphor for human life.

The speaker here seems to have more reason than Jacques for pessimism; but what shines through the poem – more brightly than any *crystal stair* – is tough, stubborn hope.

■ Read the biographical note on page 149, then the poem on an enlarged copy of photocopiable page 18. Can the children describe the kind of person who is speaking? What is there about her speech that tells us something about her personality and circumstances? Does she use standard English? Hughes was writing at a time when Black American people were viciously discriminated against, and in cities they were usually condemned to live in ghettos where housing was poor. It is evident in the poem that this woman has lived a tough life, and the tiredness in her voice and her use of 'uneducated' language *(ain't been no; I's still climbin')* emphasises this.

■ There are two 'staircases' in this poem. *Crystal stair* is a lovely phrase; can the children offer words associated with crystal – for example, *clarity* (as in *crystal clear*), *glittering*, *jewel-like*, *smooth*? Yet crystal staircases don't exist in real life; so is the mother telling her son that such a thing, such a life, is just a fantasy? Or is she suggesting that some people's lives *are* like that? If so, what sort of people? And what is the staircase like that *she* has had to climb? In what kind of building might it be?

■ Remind the children what an extended metaphor is: taking a comparison between one thing and another, and then growing other comparisons out of it (like Jacques' world being a stage metaphor). How is life 'like' climbing a staircase? Can the children see something religious in the idea? (Ascending to heaven, perhaps?) Can they suggest what might those *tacks*, *splinters* and bare, dark places be, metaphorically? How might you *fall*, or just *set down on the steps*?

■ Are the children familiar with the term *free verse* to describe poems like this? 'Mother to Son' has its own individual form or structure; can the children suggest how it is put together? (It can be divided into three parts: lines 1–7, 8–13 and 14-20. Within each part there is a pattern of repetition and short lines balanced against longer ones.) Although there is no single rhythm running through the poem, can the children hear the rhythms of natural speech in it? Can they spot how the repetition of *And* at line-beginnings suggests tired plodding, but also determination and courage?

■ Which of the following words would the class use to describe the feeling in this poem? *Bitter, sad, brave, weary, pessimistic, uncaring, defeated, optimistic, determined*? Any others?

Jacques

All the world's a stage,
And all the men and women merely players:
They have their exits and their entrances;
And one man in his time plays many parts,
His acts being seven ages. At first the infant,
Mewling and puking in the nurse's arms.
And then the whining school-boy, with his satchel
And shining morning face, creeping like snail
Unwillingly to school. And then the lover,
Sighing like furnace, with a woeful ballad
Made to his mistress' eyebrow. Then a soldier,
Full of strange oaths, and bearded like the pard,
Jealous in honour, sudden and quick in quarrel,
Seeking the bubble reputation
Even in the cannon's mouth. And then the justice,
In fair round belly with good capon lin'd,
With eyes severe, and beard of formal cut,
Full of wise saws and modern instances;
And so he plays his part. The sixth age shifts
Into the lean and slipper'd pantaloon,
With spectacles on nose and pouch on side,
His youthful hose, well sav'd, a world too wide
For his shrunk shank; and his big manly voice,
Turning again toward childish treble, pipes
And whistles in his sound. Last scene of all,
That ends this strange eventful history,
Is second childishness and mere oblivion,
Sans teeth, sans eyes, sans taste, sans everything.

from *As You Like It* by William Shakespeare

SCHOLASTIC LITERACY CENTRES

The Destruction of Sennacherib

The Assyrian came down like the wolf on the fold,
And his cohorts were gleaming in purple and gold;
And the sheen of their spears was like stars on the sea,
When the blue wave rolls nightly on deep Galilee.

Like the leaves of the forest when Summer is green,
That host with their banners at sunset were seen;
Like the leaves of the forest when Autumn hath blown,
That host on the morrow lay wither'd and strown.

For the Angel of Death spread his wings on the blast,
And breathed in the face of the foe as he pass'd;
And the eyes of the sleepers waxed deadly and chill,
And their hearts but once heaved, and for ever grew still!

And there lay the steed with his nostril all wide,
But through it there roll'd not the breath of his pride;
And the foam of his gasping lay white on the turf,
And cold as the spray of the rock-beating surf.

And there lay the rider distorted and pale,
With the dew on his brow, and the rust on his mail;
And the tents were all silent, the banners alone,
The lances unlifted, the trumpet unblown.

And the widows of Ashur are loud in their wail,
And the idols are broke in the temple of Baal;
And the might of the Gentile, unsmote by the sword,
Hath melted like snow in the glance of the Lord!

Lord Byron

Silver

Slowly, silently, now the moon

Walks the night in her silver shoon;

This way, and that, she peers, and sees

Silver fruit upon silver trees;

One by one the casements catch

Her beams beneath the silvery thatch;

Couched in his kennel, like a log,

With paws of silver sleeps the dog;

From their shadowy cote the white breasts peep

Of doves in a silver-feathered sleep;

A harvest mouse goes scampering by,

With silver claws, and silver eye;

And moveless fish in the water gleam,

By silver reeds in a silver stream.

Walter de la Mare

Mother to Son

18

Well, son, I'll tell you:

Life for me ain't been no crystal stair.

It's had tacks in it,

And splinters,

And boards torn up,

And places with no carpets on the floor -

Bare.

But all the time

I's been a-climbin' on,

And reachin' landins,

And turnin' corners,

And sometimes goin' in the dark

Where there ain't been no light.

So boy, don't you turn back.

Don't you set down on the steps

'Cause you finds it's kinder hard.

Don't you fall now -

For I's still goin', honey,

I's still climbin',

And life for me ain't been no crystal stair.

Langston Hughes

GUIDED READING NOTES

Explore the physical features of the book. What strikes the children about its appearance? The illustrations are all by the same artist, but vary enormously in style; what does this suggest about the poems themselves? What is unusual about the contents pages? What do they tell us about how the poems are sequenced? Not all collections are arranged chronologically – what other ways are there? (For example, by theme or subject; or form – limericks, story poems and so on.) Can the children suggest why Rosen decided to order this collection chronologically? (Perhaps to show how language and ways of writing have changed over the centuries, or to show how the same themes recur.) How might the two sets of notes at the end of the book help us with the poems?

Read Michael Rosen's introduction. How does he define *classic*? Have the children heard it used in different ways? Can they summarise what Rosen says in paragraphs 2, 3 and 4? What's the connection between what he says here and the portraits on the contents pages? In paragraph 6, Rosen calls English an *umbrella* word. Can the children use the word *metaphor* confidently to explain this phrase?

Read with the children the two Wordsworth poems on pages 22-3. What do the poems have in common? (They are both about taking delight in a particular place, and the sense of calm and happiness that it brings. They are both about experiencing peace.) How do the poems differ in terms of place, time and language? Explain any words and phrases, if necessary, such as *steep* (to soak or drench with light, here) and *masquerading* (going about in disguise, or going to a party where everyone wears a mask). Which poem seems 'simpler'?

The exclamation *Dear God!* (the penultimate line of the first poem) is a gasp of surprise; what has caused it? (That there can be such moments of beautiful calm in a great, bustling city.) Point out to the group that in London Wordsworth is keenly aware of silence, while in the country it is the sounds that he notices. It's the unexpectedness of each experience that fascinates him. (In both poems, the poet is out at a strange time: dawn in the city, the gathering dark in the country.)

Read with the children the note about the sonnet on page 157 and see if they can apply it to the first poem. There's a pattern of the same rhymes (*wear/bare*, *lie/sky*) in the first eight lines, and a different one (*steep/deep*, *hill/will*) in the last six. By ascribing letters to each rhyme, children should discover the pattern abba, abba, cdcdcd.

How successful is Paul Howard at conveying the mood of each poem? Which words or thoughts might his illustrations suggest? And if we were in those two places today, what else might we see? Do the children think we can experience the same sense of peacefulness that Wordsworth felt 200 years ago?

19

CONT. . .

purple/blue

Poetry

CONT. . .

SCHOLASTIC LITERACY CENTRES

20

Read 'A Bird came down the Walk' by Emily Dickinson (page 78), then the biographical note. Emily Dickinson died alone and relatively unknown. Only seven of her brilliant poems were published during her lifetime – all the rest were published after her death.

She had a fantastic gift for metaphor; and quite often – as in this poem – she'd save the big metaphor until the end, so that many of her poems have a dramatic 'twist in the tail' which takes us into an unexpected realm. For most of this poem, she's sharing with us a fairly jokey (*the fellow; convenient; To let a beetle pass*) look at a bird. Does the group recognise this 'observational portrait' of a bird? But then, at the end,

she springs a new idea on us, and this has to do with seeing flying as like swimming or boating. Can the children pick out the key words which introduce this metaphor? The word *rowed* is the first, suggesting similarity in the motions of wings and oars, and this unlocks the idea of air as water, the sky as an ocean or river, in that incredibly beautiful last stanza in which butterflies *swim*. Try exploring the meaning of *Banks*: the sloping sides of a valley, hedges, the sides of a river. Is Dickinson picturing the noonday light, between two slopes, as a river? And why *plashless*? How does that missing *s* soften or 'dry' the sound, and why?

What do children notice about Dickinson's use of punctuation (those odd dashes) and capital letters? Does its eccentricity make the poem harder to read, or not?

Ask the children to read Tennyson's 'The Eagle' (page 55). Can they express what Tennyson is saying about this bird, compared to the Dickinson poem? (The Eagle is all about power and superiority, whereas Dickinson's bird is far more human – nervous, busy and eager to get off home.)

Now read Emily Dickinson's 'The Wind' (page 81). Personification is the main metaphorical 'trick' in this poem. Can the children remember what it means and give examples from the poem? The word *Hands* is significant – what sort and size of hands? Human-sized ones? No – Dickinson seems to be suggesting that when there's a storm the sky is full of giants.

The poem is about a storm breaking; how do the pace and the language help to convey this sense of something building? Can the children see that Dickinson darts from one thing to the next, hardly ever using more than two lines to sketch each event? Look at the words in terms of syllables; only one word in the entire poem has more than two (*quartering* in the last line), and this attracts our attention to it. And what does it mean? That the storm split the tree into four? Yes, but *quarter* has other meanings, one of which is 'to range about like hunting dogs seeking a scent', so perhaps the storm is deliberately hunting for a victim.

Dickinson was a deeply religious woman; with that in mind, what two meanings might *my Father's House* have? Is there perhaps a religious 'message' in the poem?

You might compare this high-energy piece with Christina Rossetti's vapid little poem on the next page.

Read 'He Wishes for the Cloths of Heaven' by WB Yeats (page 116). In this famous love poem, Yeats uses ideas which are both simple and fantastical; the sky and his dreams become physical, concrete things upon which his lover can walk. The word *Heaven* in the title has obvious religious connotations, but can the children work out that here these *cloths* are the skies, *embroidered* or *Enwrought* with the sun, moon and stars? Can they enjoy the mad but lovely image of someone pulling down the sky, like curtains, and laying it on the ground to make a carpet for a lover's feet? What is strange about *But I, being poor*? Does the poet believe that rich people *could* buy the sky? Or is this ironic? Is he suggesting that

dreams like his are more valuable than mere wealth?

Discuss with the children the different kinds of repetition Yeats uses to pattern his language, which gives it a rhythm that is sometimes chant-like. Most obvious are the line-endings; the use of identical rhyme (using the same word twice) is sometimes considered 'cheating' or feeble, but here it is deliberate and purposeful. There is alliteration in lines 1 and 3, and internal rhymes in lines 4 and 7. An insistent beat is created in lines 3 and 4 by repeating *and* and *and the*; *tread* is used twice in the last line. Rhythmically, the lines all have four strong beats (easiest to count in lines 3 and 4), except for the last line. So although this poem has a rather trance-like and unworldly quality, it achieves it through language which is not only beautiful but also very disciplined and strongly patterned.

And what does that last line mean? What interpretations can the group offer?

Read 'Arithmetic' by Carl Sandburg (pages 136–7). This is a long way from those densely structured poems by Walter de La Mare and WB Yeats. But there is one use of repetition here – each paragraph begins with either *Arithmetic* or *If*.

Sandburg is writing 'in role'; who's voice might this be? This is a fun piece, of course, and we wouldn't want to make heavy weather of it. But can the children work out that this poem is about the sense of confusion and inadequacy we experience when confronted by something we don't really understand? (We sometimes use an arithmetical expression for this incomprehension: things *don't add up*.) Can the children express the way Sandburg uses language to convey this feeling? Can they see how the speaker plunges into those long, garbled, unpunctuated sentences with (apparently) no idea where they might end up? And that in the penultimate paragraph there's a distinct, surreal note of hysteria? It all ends optimistically, though; what does that last paragraph suggest? (That sometimes it's a stroke of luck when someone can't count.)

Like Langston Hughes's 'Mother to Son', this is a free verse poem. You could direct children to a much earlier free verse poem, Walt Whitman's 'I Hear America Singing' (pages 72–3), which is also a sort of progression or list. Can the children see that unlike Sandburg, Whitman is celebrating things in a completely unironic way?

ACTIVITY NOTES

Performing poems

Objectives: to understand the dramatic elements in some classic poems; to share and collaborate in reading them.

Resources: copies of *The Walker Book of Classic Poetry and Poets*.

Activity: Choose a selection of poems from the book for performance. 'Performance' can mean anything from expressive reading to physical enactment. Performing is easier when reading poems with both narrative voice and speaker(s), so you could start with, for example, Edgar Allan Poe's 'Eldorado' (page 53), Lewis Carroll's 'Jabberwocky' (pages 88–9) and Walter de la Mare's 'The Listeners' (page 125–7). However, assigning stanzas, rather than 'parts', to individuals can work just as well.

Ideally, the class or group should always polish the reading of a poem by means of constructive criticism and participation. The Shakespeare pieces (pages 12–15), for example, require dramatisation, since they are from plays; the group should see itself as a director working with whoever is chosen to be the actor/reader.

The great benefit of performing poems is that children can be motivated by their responsibility to others to read and speak to the best of their abilities.

Reading chorally

Objective: to work as a group to find the music in classic poetry.

Resources: copies of *The Walker Book of Classic Poetry and Poets*, a cassette player and tape.

Activity: Organise choral readings of some of the poems. Obviously, those which approach chant or song lend themselves most readily to choral reading, whether or not they have an actual chorus or refrain. You might like to try William Blake's 'The Tyger' (pages 17–19), Lewis Carroll's 'The Mock Turtle's Song' (pages 84–6), the anonymous 'Swing Low, Sweet Chariot' (page 91), Robert Louis Stevenson's 'From a Railway Carriage' (page 98), Banjo Paterson's 'Waltzing Matilda' (pages 104–6) and Rudyard Kipling's 'A Smuggler's Song' (pages 110–11).

You will almost certainly find that the natural rhythms of the poems emerge when children try to co-ordinate and time their ensemble readings. From time to time, record the class or group reading chorally, to facilitate (cheerful) self-criticism.

Poems by heart

Objective: to memorise poems.

Resources: copies of *The Walker Book of Classic Poetry and Poets*.

Activity: Although considered by some to be old-fashioned and quaint, learning poems by heart is actually very worthwhile. Apart from exercising memory and expanding vocabulary, learning poems is a fine way of appreciating the importance of rhythm in poetry. Children will quickly understand that one of the functions of regular rhythm is to aid memorability, and that the stronger the beat in a poem the easier it is to remember the words (something which is essential to narrative poetry). And children get a great kick out of successfully learning something all the way through.

Give the children some poems to learn by heart. The poems suggested for choral reading above are all memorable, as is, for example, Lewis Carroll's 'How Doth the Little Crocodile' (page 87).

Compiling a glossary

Objectives: to tackle unfamiliar words; to deduce meanings from contexts; to use dictionaries; to share learning with others.

Resources: copies of *The Walker Book of Classic Poetry and Poets*, dictionaries, a ring-binder (optional), paper, writing materials.

Activity: Michael Rosen explains words such as *billabong* and *magi* in his notes at the back of *The Walker Book of Classic Poetry and Poets* in order to help younger readers to understand the poems better. As an ongoing activity for your class, compile a glossary of other unfamiliar words encountered in the collection.

The glossary of new and unfamiliar words compiled by the children could be 'handed down' to the next class who come to read *The Walker Book of Classic Poetry and Poets*. Those children might add to or reorganise the glossary – for example, if the words are in page order, they could rearrange them into alphabetical order. They may choose to add extra information or illustrations.

Such a glossary or poetical dictionary should be a special thing, an opportunity for discussing and producing 'best' writing. And if there are children for whom writing is not their greatest strength, they might enjoy activities such as illustrating the glossary, designing it and collating it, perhaps placing the finished product in an attractive ring-binder.

Poet quiz

Objectives: to become familiar with the organisation of the core text; to scan texts in order to locate particular items of information; to gain familiarity with the lives of classic poets.

Resources: photocopiable page 29, copies of *The Walker Book of Classic Poetry and Poets*, writing materials. Optional – bag (or box), scissors.

Activity: Initiate this activity whenever you think it most appropriate. You might want to use it early on to familiarise children with the way the book is structured, or you may prefer to use it after shared or guided reading when the group should be a little more familiar with the book and how to find information in it. The children can locate the answers in the contents pages, the biographical notes on the poets, and the two sets of notes at the back of the book. The answers are: 1. 83; 2. 36, in Greece; 3. Lewis Carroll; 4. Edgar Allan Poe; 5. six years; 6. Emily Dickinson; 7. Carl Sandburg, John Masefield, Siegfried Sassoon and Langston Hughes all died that year; 8. He drowned at sea off the coast of Italy, 30; 9. Andrew Barton; 10. New York state in USA; 11. Coleridge; 12. ballad.

You could turn this activity into a game. Cut the photocopiable sheet into individual strips and put them into a bag or box. Divide the group into two teams and ask each team to draw out six questions; the team with the first correct answers wins.

Anthology

Objectives: to find poems and record information about the poets; to use *The Walker Book of Classic Poetry and Poets* as a model for compiling a class anthology.

Resources: photocopiable page 30, books of poetry and ICT reference sources, writing, drawing and colouring materials.

Activity: The photocopiable sheet is a template of a poem plus potted biography page from *The Walker Book of Classic Poetry and Poets*; the class or group should use it to build its own anthology. The use of the template should help to give the end-product a more consistent and 'professional' appearance, as well as giving the children a structure for their work. Ask the children to find and transcribe poems by:
■ classic poets not in the collection, for example Robert Burns, Wilfred Owen, *or*
■ modern classic poets, for example Ogden Nash, Stevie Smith, Ted Hughes, Jack Prelutsky, *or*
■ favourite contemporary poets.

For each anthology page, they should fill in the title of the poem in the space provided, followed by the poem itself, then research and write a short biography of, or comment on, the poet in the narrower left-hand column, along with a drawing of the poet, if possible.

Seven ages

Objectives: to understand and adapt the structure of a poem and devise new vocabulary.
Resources: photocopiable page 31, copies of *The Walker Book of Classic Poetry and Poets*, writing, drawing and colouring materials, extra paper if necessary.
Activity: Re-read Jacques' speech in *The Walker Book of Classic Poetry and Poets* (pages 12–13), referring to the illustration as a visual summary of the seven stages of a man's life. Discuss, as a group, how a *modern* man's or woman's life might be similarly summarised.

Now ask the children to work individually or in pairs on the photocopiable sheet. They should label each stage, as shown for *baby*, and compile verbs and adjectives which might apply to it. Six words per box would be a reasonable target, and rhyming words would be a bonus. Children might want to include small illustrations, or make their own versions of Paul Howard's 'grid' picture on a separate sheet.
Extension: Encourage the children to write a short poem of their own about the seven ages of a person by selecting and developing words from their completed photocopiable sheets and linking them, as Shakespeare does, with simple connectives, for example *then, and then, fourthly, lastly*. Rhyme is optional. You may decide to work with a group to achieve this objective. A possible opening might be:

A woman has seven ages. First the baby
Gurgling and burbling, snug in her pram;
Next, the toddler...

Marking the beat

Objective: to see how stressed and unstressed syllables are used to create rhythms in regular classic poetry.
Resources: photocopiable page 32, copies of *The Walker Book of Classic Poetry and Poets*, writing materials, including coloured pencils or felt-tipped pens.
Activity: Read 'The Tyger' by William Blake (pages 17–19). The photocopiable sheet reprints the first two stanzas with the first four lines divided into individual syllables,

and some lines marked to indicate stressed syllables ('beats') and unstressed syllables. Filled circles have been used for stressed syllables and blank circles for unstressed ones, but the children might like to devise their own methods of marking, inventing their own symbols or perhaps using two different-coloured pencils or felt-tipped pens.

Children should discover a pattern – that is, rhythm – emerging. These will not be *exactly* regular (hardly any poems are perfectly regular because that would be too boring and unnatural).

When the activity has been completed, read the marked verses with the group, beating or clapping out the beats.

Extension: Introduce the word *scansion*, or *scanning*, to name this activity of investigating the rhythms of regular verse. Other poems in *The Walker Book of Classic Poetry and Poets* which have very clear and predictable scansion include Thomas Hood's 'The Song of the Shirt' (pages 35–9), Robert Louis Stevenson's 'From a Railway Carriage' (page 98) and Rudyard Kipling's 'A Smuggler's Song' (pages 110–11).

Point out that two of these poems have *song* in their titles; this strongly indicates that the more regular and beat-driven a poem is, the more it starts to resemble music. If you feel able to, you could try a rap-style reading of 'From a Railway Carriage' to reinforce this point.

Sort out a sonnet

Objectives: to secure understanding of what a rhyme scheme is; to arrange the lines of a sonnet in the right order.

Resources: photocopiable page 33, copies of *The Walker Book of Classic Poetry and Poets*, writing materials, flip chart or board, scissors, glue, paper.

Activity: Briefly revisit Wordsworth's 'Sonnet composed upon Westminster Bridge, 3rd September 1802' (page 22) and remind the children that a sonnet has 14 lines arranged in a certain pattern of rhymes, or rhyme scheme. Wordsworth's follows the abba, abba, cdcdcd rhyme scheme. Explain that this is just one pattern for sonnets, and that the sonnet the children are going to play with has one that is a bit different. At this point, collect in copies of the book.

The lines from Shelley's sonnet 'Ozymandias' (page 30) have been muddled up on the photocopiable sheet. Ask the children if they can put the lines in the correct order so that they make sense and the rhymes fit together. The poem has been rearranged into seven groups of two sequential lines. (Thus the task may be differentiated according to ability: cutting the page into single lines is quite challenging; cutting it into pairs less so.) The first two lines on the photocopiable sheet are the first two lines of the poem. If you want to provide further help, write the rhyme scheme on the board: abab, acdc, edfgfg.

Ask the children to paste their rejigged texts onto sheets of paper. How do they compare to the original?

A sad knight

Objectives: to use explanatory notes and a glossary to enhance understanding of a text; to explore the ballad form; to summarise a narrative; to comment on the mood of a text and illustration.

Resources: photocopiable page 34, copies of *The Walker Book of Classic Poetry and Poets*, writing, drawing and colouring materials, paper.
Activity: First read Keats' 'La Belle Dame Sans Merci' (pages 32–4). Don't translate the title, ask the children how they might find out what it means. There is a note on the poem (page 154) and a brief explanation of the ballad form (page 157). This information should enable the children to complete the first part of the photocopiable sheet. The last two lines of the first stanza should be stressed:

The/sedge/has/with/ered/from/the/lake

And/no/birds/sing.

The glossary at the foot of the sheet should help the children with the story, although they will almost certainly have to guess at or deduce the meaning of some words.

The children are asked to illustrate part of the poem; they will need not only to visualise the poem but to decide how they might reflect its *mood*; encourage them to think about colour, in particular. The image of the ghostly victims (stanzas 10 and 11) should provide a stimulus for some children.

Another helping of Calico Pie

Objectives: to investigate nonsense verse; to write extension verses of a poem, using the poem's structure.
Resources: copies of *The Walker Book of Classic Poetry and Poets*, writing materials.
Activity: Read Edward Lear's 'Calico Pie' (pages 58–9). You may need to explain that *calico* is white cotton cloth – so we are in the realm of nonsense verse, here. Ask the children to write new verses to the poem, keeping to the rhyme pattern and line length. The same refrain (the last four lines) should be used, so just six new lines per verse need to be invented.

Point out that the activity involves thinking of two rhymes, and the children will need to structure their new verses as follows:
■ two lines that rhyme
■ then a line ending in an *ee* sound
■ followed by three lines that rhyme
■ then the refrain.
Extension: Work as a group or class to polish the additional verses; illustrate them and add them to the class anthology.

Metaphor links

Objectives: to perceive and develop patterns of metaphor and use them in personal writing.
Resources: photocopiable page 35, copies of *The Walker Book of Classic Poetry and Poets*, writing materials.
Activity: Revisit, if necessary, 'The Wind' by Emily Dickinson (page 81). Can the children spot that the first 'word chain' on the photocopiable sheet consists of words from the poem which all relate to its central metaphor (wind as hands)? Encourage

them to use their imaginations to complete the word chains for the other four subjects. Three of these give the central metaphor (in the rectangular boxes): mist is a cat, rain is glass, a forest fire is a dragon. The words the children write in each of the 'links' should be ones associated with the word in the rectangular box. The children need to think of their own metaphor for river. (*Snake* is a fairly obvious one if they need a suggestion.)

Extension: Ask the children to use the back of the sheet to turn one or two of their word chains into complete sentences. More confident writers might be challenged not to use the word *like* – in other words, not to write similes. These sentences might in turn be developed into short poems.

How doth the...?

Objectives: to see the relationship between a parody and its original, and to write a parody of a given text.

Resources: photocopiable page 36, copies of *The Walker Book of Classic Poetry and Poets*, the poem 'Against Idleness and Mischief' by Isaac Watts (optional), writing materials.

Activity: Read the note on parody (page 157) to the children, then read the first two stanzas of Isaac Watts' poem 'Against Idleness and Mischief', provided here.

> *How doth the little busy Bee*
> *   Improve each shining Hour,*
> *And gather Honey all the day*
> *   From every opening Flower!*
>
> *How skilfully she builds her Cell!*
> *   How neat she spreads the Wax!*
> *And labours hard to store it well*
> *   With the sweet Food she makes.*

Read the rest of the poem, if you have it available, and briefly discuss it. Explain that Issac Watts lived in the 17th century (1674–1768). Try to ensure that the children grasp the didactic, moralistic nature of the poem.

Next, read Lewis Carroll's parody of Watts on page 87. This parody is just cheeky and funny, rather than hostile and cruel as some parodies are. To be recognised as such, parodies need to retain elements of the original; can the children spot them? Rhythm is especially important here.

The photocopiable sheet offers Carroll's poem with space for writing between each line. The children should work towards their own parodies of this parody by crossing out words and substituting new ones and seeing where that takes them. (For example, *How doth the little busy flea/Annoy each shining cat?*) By writing between the lines of the poem, they may be able to maintain the rhythm of the original.

Extension: Writing parodies is a good way of getting to grips with a poem's form and language. Children might try parodying single stanzas of William Blake's 'The Tyger' (pages 17–19) or Lewis Carroll's 'Jabberwocky' (pages 88–9). Christina Rossetti's 'Who has seen the wind?' (page 82) is simple to parody: 'Who has seen the dinner lady?' perhaps, or 'Who has seen the burger van/caretaker/headteacher/my trainers?'

Waltzing Matilda

Objectives: to use notes and a glossary; to introduce new language into a poem while conforming to its structure.

Resources: copies of *The Walker Book of Classic Poetry and Poets*, paper, writing materials.

Activity: Read 'Waltzing Matilda' by Banjo Paterson (pages 104–6). What tells us that it's a song, even if we've never heard it? (The regular rhythm, and the presence of a chorus.) See if the children can deduce from the context the meanings of the Australian words. (The illustrations should help greatly.) Using their previous knowledge of *The Walker Book of Classic Poetry and Poets*, can the children check the definitions they've offered? (The notes are on page 156. You could point out that Rosen doesn't explain the poem's title. A *Matilda* is a backpack, and to *waltz matilda* is to walk carrying one.)

Now ask the children to write out the first four lines of the first and second stanzas, replacing the Australianisms with conventional English words. What is the major problem they encounter? What happens to the rhythm of the poem if they simply substitute the glossary definitions? Can they see that they need to match *syllables* as well as meanings? What new words can they offer? And why can't we Anglicise *coolibah*?

Extension: Ask a group to 'translate' the whole poem, and write its story in prose. Then read it to the class or another group. What gets lost?

Visualise

Objective: to illustrate a poem, showing awareness of its subject and mood through careful reading.

Resources: copies of *The Walker Book of Classic Poetry and Poets*, paper, writing and drawing materials.

Activity: Select a poem from the anthology which is not illustrated – for example, Tennyson's 'The Eagle' and 'Break, Break, Break' (page 55), Walt Whitman's 'Mannahatta' (page 74) and 'Miracles' (page 75), Rudyard Kipling's 'The Way Through the Woods' (page 113), Robert Frost's 'The Road Not Taken' (page 129). Or choose a poem with minimal illustration, such as John Clare's 'Clock-a-Clay' (page 31) or Thomas Hardy's 'Throwing a Tree' (page 94),

Ask the children to draw their own illustrations for the selected poem. They should read it carefully, paying particularly attention to the *mood* of the poem and thinking about image (which particular lines of the poem will they focus on?) and colour. For example, 'Miracles' is joyous and celebratory, whereas 'Break, Break, Break' is sombre and grieving. What colour scheme might be appropriate to each? Will the illustration take up a full page – like, for example, Hilaire Belloc's 'Tarantella' (page 123)? Or will the illustration be integral to the poem – such as in Edward Lear's 'Calico Pie' (pages 58–9)?

Encourage children who are not confident about drawing to write a description of the picture they might draw or make simple sketches.

Extension: Ask the children to use their drawings, notes and sketches to produce finished illustrations. Compile these along with the poems they illustrate to form an illustrated class anthology.

Name   Date

Poet quiz

1. How old was Judith Wright when *The Walker Book of Classic Poetry and Poets* was published?

2. How old was Lord Byron when he died, and where did he die?

3. Whose real name was Charles Lutwidge Dodgson?

4. Which poet is most famous for writing horror stories?

5. For how many years did John Keats write poetry?

6. Who wrote over 2000 poems but only lived to see 7 of them printed?

7. Why was 1967 a sad year for poetry lovers?

8. How did Shelley die, and how old was he?

9. What were Banjo Patterson's real first names?

10. Where did the Iroquois live?

11. Who said that his poem came to him in a dream, but was interrupted by a visitor before he could write it all down?

12. In Elizabethan times, poems were sold at fairs, in pubs and on the streets. What is this sort of poem called?

Name

Date

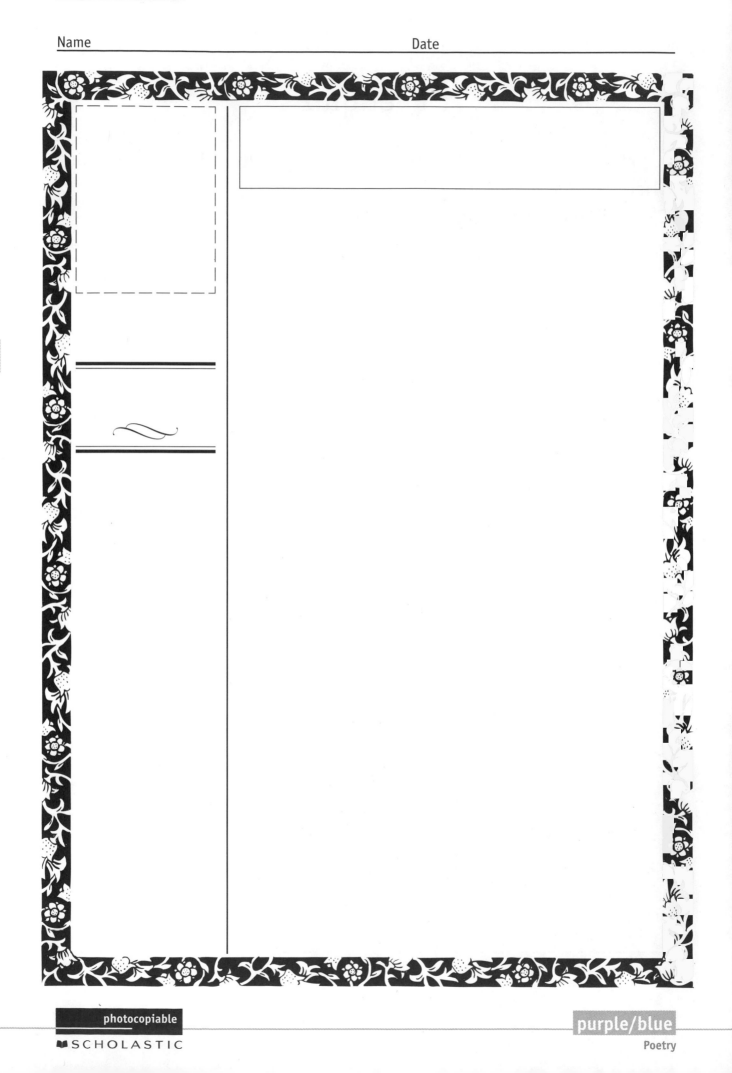

Name _____ Date _____

Seven ages

How did Jacques summarise the seven stages of a man's life (page 12)?
Write your own version for a modern man or woman here. Can you
illustrate it too?

The seven ages of a modern…	1 **Baby:** gurgle, burble
2	3
4	5
6	7

Name _____   Date _____

Marking the beat

These are the first two stanzas of William Blake's 'The Tyger'. Some of the lines have been divided into syllables, and some have the 'beat' syllables marked with a black dot and the light syllables marked with a white dot. Try to divide and mark the other lines. (You could use colours, if you prefer.) Can you see patterns emerging?

Illustration © 1998 Paul Howard

Ty|ger!|Ty|ger!|burn|ing|bright

In|the|for|ests|of|the|night,
● ○ ● ○ ● ○ ●

What|im|mort|al|hand|or|eye

Could|frame|thy|fear|ful|sym|met|ry?
○ ● ○ ● ○ ● ○ ●

In what distant deeps or skies

Burnt|the|fi|re|of|thine|eyes?
● ○ ● ○ ○ ○ ●

On what wings dare he aspire?

What the hand dare seize the fire?

Name   Date

Sort out a sonnet

This sonnet doesn't make much sense because its lines are in a muddle.
Cut them out and try to get them in the right order. Remember that
sonnets have a rhyme scheme, so juggle the lines until you find a pattern of
rhymes appearing and the poem makes sense.

I met a traveller from an antique land

Who said: Two vast and trunkless legs of stone

Look on my works, ye Mighty, and despair!"

Nothing beside remains. Round the decay

And wrinkled lip, and sneer of cold command,

Tell that its sculptor well those passions read

And on the pedestal these words appear:

"My name is Ozymandias, king of kings;

Stand in the desert. Near them, on the sand,

Half sunk, a shattered visage lies, whose frown,

Of that colossal wreck, boundless and bare,

The lone and level sands stretch far away.

Which yet survive (stamped on those lifeless things),

The hand that mocked them and the heart that fed;

Name _____ Date _____

A sad knight

The poem by Keats on page 32 of *The Walker Book of Classic Poetry and Poets* is called 'La Belle Dame Sans Merci'.

1. What does that mean in English?

_____

2. What kind of poem is it?

_____

3. Divide the third and fourth lines into syllables and mark the ones that are **beats**.

O what can ail thee, knight-at-arms,
Alone and palely loitering?

> The sedge has withered from the lake,

> And no birds sing.

4. Tell the story of the poem in a few sentences.

_____

_____

_____

_____

5. Who, or what, do you think the Belle Dame is, really?

_____

6. Comment on the illustration. Does it suit the mood of the poem?

_____

_____

_____

_____

7. How would *you* illustrate the poem? Which part would you illustrate? Do your illustration on a separate sheet of paper.

Glossary

ail trouble	**sedge** reeds	**zone** belt or sash	**grot** grotto or cave
thrall the power of a magic spell	**starved** freezing	**sojourn** time spent alone

---

Name

Date

Metaphor links

Complete these word chains.

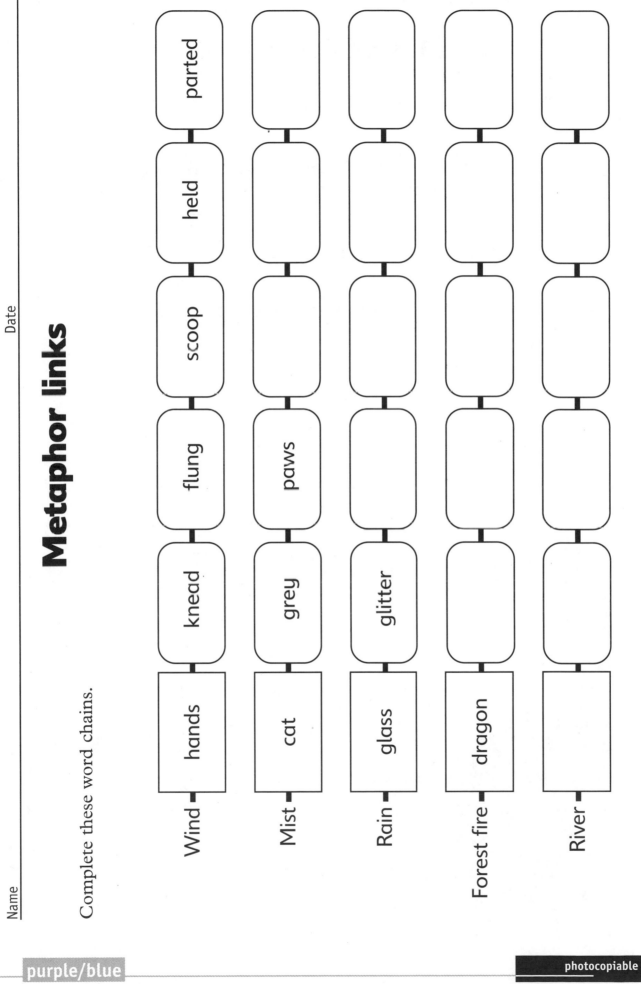

Wind	hands	knead	flung	scoop	held	parted
Mist	cat	grey	paws			
Rain	glass	glitter				
Forest fire	dragon					
River						

Name

Date

How doth the...?

Write your own parody of Lewis Carroll's poem.

How doth the little crocodile

_____

Improve his shining tail,

_____

And pour the waters of the Nile

_____

On every golden scale!

_____

How cheerfully he seems to grin,

_____

How neatly spreads his claws,

_____

And welcomes little fishes in

_____

With gently smiling jaws!

_____

Illustration © 1998 Paul Howard

Amazon.com® book review

Background

This short review is conventional in that it is a mix of information, opinion and value judgement. As readers, it's important that we are able to tell which is which, of course. This particular review is taken from the Internet – from the website of the booksellers Amazon. That fact should make a difference to the way we read it. We might value objectivity and impartiality in a review, but this is written for and published by a company wanting to sell *The Walker Book of Classic Poetry and Poets*. It is an advertisement in disguise.

Booksellers' and publishers' websites can be useful playgrounds for children. A number of them – including Amazon – encourage children to add their own reviews of books they have read: a fine opportunity for 'writing with a purpose', and a simple way to get published.

■ Read through the text on photocopiable page 39. What tells us that it is from the Internet, from an American bookseller's website? Explain that an 'editorial review', in this instance, is one written for Amazon by someone who works for the company.

■ Take a close look at the language. There are several tricky words and sentences. *Hearty* usually has to do with food – what's it doing here? *Chameleonic* is a strange word – what is it about Paul Howard's work that reminds the writer of a chameleon? What does the word *treasury* make us think of? In the quote from Michael Rosen, he uses the word *springboard* – what particular trick of language is that (metaphor), and what idea does it express? Can the children work out what the reviewer means by *artwork styles that complement the moods and historical context of each poem*? How would they rewrite that phrase to make it more easily understood?

■ Parts of this text give us actual information; other parts give us... what? The review is written anonymously – does this make us less or more likely to accept the reviewer's opinion? Is there anything critical in this review? So what is it trying to do? Is it really a review at all? If not, what is it?

■ This text is about a children's book – is the text itself 'child-friendly'? Do the children agree with what's in this text? Is there anything they might argue with (for example, *...to the modern day* at the end of the third sentence)? Are there things they would have mentioned that the reviewer hasn't? The three photocopiable sheets offer children an approach to organising and writing their own reviews of *The Walker Book of Classic Poetry and Poets*.

■ Photocopiable page 40 simply asks children to make and justify a choice of poets and poems to cite in a review. They may choose ones they happen to like, which is fine; but you might suggest other criteria, such as representing the historical and/or international scope of the collection, or its variety.

■ Photocopiable page 41 is a sequence of question prompts directed towards compiling the content of the review. The children should write notes or brief sentences in the appropriate panels. In the section *What are the unusual features of the book?* they should suggest the illustrated contents pages, the portraits and 'potted biographies' in the text, and the notes and explanations at the back.

CONT. . .

37

CONT. . .

■ Photocopiable page 42, more challengingly, asks children to condense their notes and opinions into the format of a brief review similar to the extra text. They should try to cover all the topics indicated. The *Book information* panel needs title, author, illustrator, publisher, ISBN and price.

■ Children might want to write parts of their reviews and send them to websites such as Amazon, BOL (Books on Line) or WH Smith.

assessment

ASSESSMENT NOTES

The things people say

Assessment focus: to express personal tastes and views; to respond to and build on the opinions of others; to discuss the enduring appeal of classic poetry.
Resources: photocopiable page 43, writing materials.
Activity: This is an individual activity to be undertaken without reference to the book. Ensure that the children read and think about *all* the quotations before beginning to write a response to one of them. Encourage them to think of particular poems as a way of responding, perhaps noting these down on the photocopiable sheet as they read through it. For example, a response to quotation 6 about slushiness might cite Byron's 'The Destruction of Sennacherib' (as might a response to quotation 4). Some children might find it easier to write two shorter responses to two different quotations.

Dream variations

Assessment focus: to write a short response to a poem, trying to express its overall effect; to consider what the poet might have been trying to achieve; to use a few technical terms correctly and with confidence.
Resources: photocopiable page 44, paper, writing materials, copies of *The Walker Book of Classic Poetry and Poets* (optional).
Activity: Children should attempt this activity individually, although you may choose to read it aloud to the group first. They should use the page to annotate the poem and jot down their thoughts, as shown. They should be able to say something about rhythm and how it varies (for example, by comparing the third line of each stanza) and something about rhyme and repetition. It would be good if (tipped off by the word *dance*) they realised that this is a very musical piece. (You might try fitting a tune to it afterwards.) They should spot that (as the title tells us) the second stanza is a *variation* on the first and identify the changes. They should grasp that contrast (between energy and rest, light and dark) is the theme, and that darkness, blackness is a welcome, positive thing. More able children might work out why this poem is a 'dream'; like Martin Luther King's, it's a dream of Black and White being equally valued, and that Hughes uses day and night as a metaphor for *people*.

Amazon.com® book review

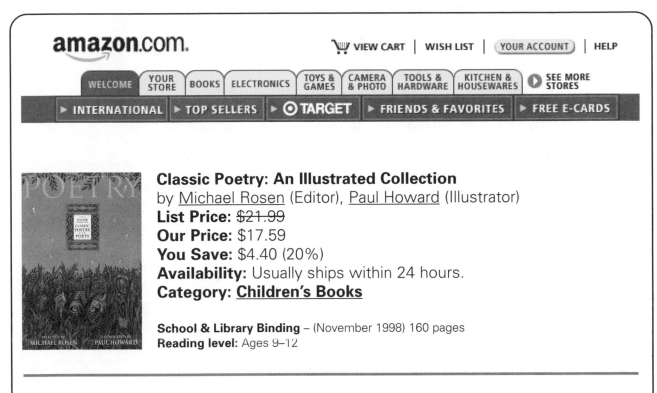

amazon.com.   🛒 **VIEW CART** | **WISH LIST** | **YOUR ACCOUNT** | **HELP**

WELCOME | YOUR STORE | BOOKS | ELECTRONICS | TOYS & GAMES | CAMERA & PHOTO | TOOLS & HARDWARE | KITCHEN & HOUSEWARES | ▶ SEE MORE STORES

▶ INTERNATIONAL | ▶ TOP SELLERS | ◎ TARGET | ▶ FRIENDS & FAVORITES | ▶ FREE E-CARDS

Classic Poetry: An Illustrated Collection
by <u>Michael Rosen</u> (Editor), <u>Paul Howard</u> (Illustrator)
List Price: ~~$21.99~~
Our Price: $17.59
You Save: $4.40 (20%)
Availability: Usually ships within 24 hours.
Category: <u>Children's Books</u>

School & Library Binding – (November 1998) 160 pages
Reading level: Ages 9–12

Editorial Reviews

Amazon.com

In so many classic poetry selections, you'll find old favourites, but no information on the creators themselves. In Michael Rosen's hearty, well-designed, 160-page anthology – with strikingly diverse illustrations by the talented and chameleonic artist Paul Howard – readers will find a portrait and short biography of each poet accompanying his or her work. Not only that but the selections are arranged chronologically, from the 17th century to the modern day. William Shakespeare's "All the World's a Stage" from *As You Like It* begins the classic collection, then readers are introduced to William Blake, Elizabeth Barrett Browning, Edward Lear, Emily Dickinson, Lewis Carroll, Langston Hughes, and many, many more. Poet, storyteller, broadcaster, and children's book author Rosen says of his treasury, "There are so many ways to enjoy poems. This book is a way of offering new insights into poems, poets, and the relationships between them. It also offers a springboard to children and adults wanting to find out more and explore the world of poetry." And illustrator Howard should take a bow for his successful efforts to explore different techniques and artwork styles that complement the moods and historical context of each poem so perfectly. We welcome the chance to revisit Lear's "The Jumblies", Longfellow's "Paul Revere's Ride", and other well-loved poems in such a beautiful package. (Ages 9 and older)

39

SCHOLASTIC LITERACY CENTRES

Name _____   Date _____

Pick your poets, pick your poems

In the Amazon review:

❏ How many poets are mentioned? _____

❏ How many poems are named? _____

If you were writing the review, which poets and poems would you mention as being specially interesting? Pick three of each, and say why you chose them.

Poets

My first poet is:

because

My second poet is:

because

My third poet is:

because

Poems

My first poem is:

because

My second poem is:

because

My third poem is:

because

SCHOLASTIC LITERACY CENTRES

40

extra text

Name _____ Date _____

Review planner

Imagine a magazine or website has asked you to write a review of *The Walker Book of Classic Poetry and Poets*. Where do you start? By following this question trail! Make notes or write short sentences in each panel.

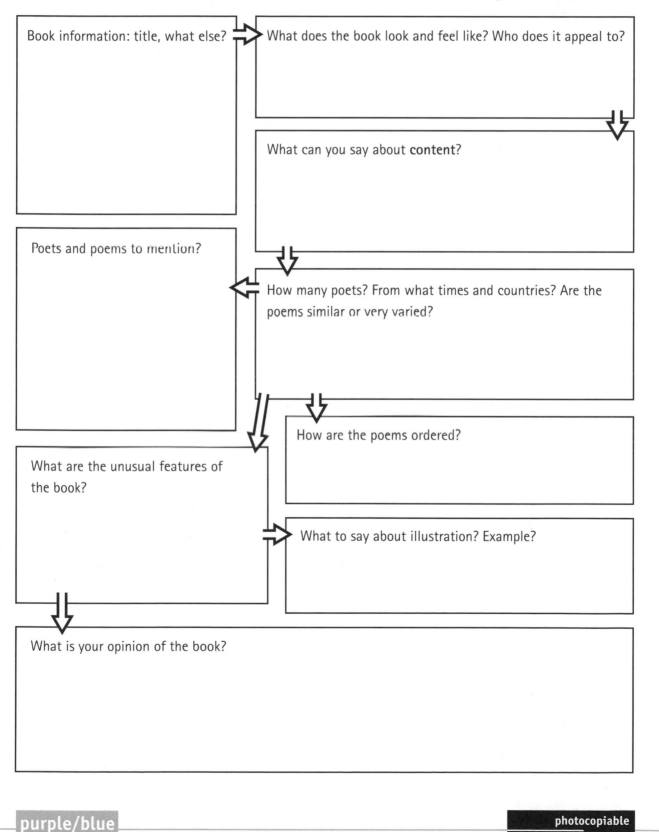

Book information: title, what else?

What does the book look and feel like? Who does it appeal to?

What can you say about **content**?

Poets and poems to mention?

How many poets? From what times and countries? Are the poems similar or very varied?

How are the poems ordered?

What are the unusual features of the book?

What to say about illustration? Example?

What is your opinion of the book?

Name

Date

My review

Reviewers often have to squeeze a lot into a small space. Use this layout to shape your review of *The Walker Book of Classic Poetry and Poets*. Try to deal with all the topics mentioned.

Book information

Appearance and appeal

Range and sequence

Unusual features

Rosen

Illustration

Opinion

■SCHOLASTIC

purple/blue

Poetry

SCHOLASTIC LITERACY CENTRES

Name _____ Date _____

The things people say

Here are some things that people have said about the kind of poetry you have been reading. You might agree or disagree with them. On the other side of the sheet, write what you would say if you were having a discussion with one of these people. Try to mention particular poems.

1. Learning a poem by heart is the best way of liking it, but you have to like it at the first glance to want to learn it by heart.

    Sir John Betjeman, poet

2. I don't like old poetry. What's the point of having to read something lots of times just to understand the words? Poetry is something you should understand first time.

    Ronan, aged 9

3. Who decides what poems are classic, anyway? It's just the people who keep putting the same ones in the books, isn't it?

    Amy, aged 10

4. I like a good poem, one with lots of fighting in it. Blood, and the clanging of armour.

    Roger McGough, from 'A Good Poem'

5. It's the rhythm, I think. You look at something in the book and go "What?" Then someone reads it out so you can hear the beat, and you think "Oh, yeah, I get it."

    Michael, aged 10

6. The trouble with a lot of classic poetry is that it's slushy. Sentimental stuff about love and nature and all that.

    Hannah, college student

Name　　　　　　　　　　　　　　　Date

Illustration © 1998 Paul Howard

44

Dream variations

Write a short piece about this poem. What is it about? What does it make you feel? What are the patterns in it? Begin by making notes on this page like the ones shown.

To fling my arms wide,

In some place of the sun,

To whirl and to dance

Till the white day is done,　　*contrast*

Then rest at cool evening

Beneath a tall tree

While night comes on gently,

Dark like me, –

That is my dream!　　*doesn't rhyme with other words. Sticks out. Why?*

To fling my arms wide,

In the face of the sun,

Dance! whirl! whirl!

Till the quick day is done,

Rest at pale evening...

A tall, slim tree...

Night coming tenderly,　　*darkness is kind*

　　Black like me.

Langston Hughes

HE THIRTEEN SECRETS OF POETRY
BY ADRIAN MITCHELL
AND VALERIE LITTLEWOOD

About the book

This is an unusual anthology. Its title intrigues, being both mysterious and oddly precise. Are there 'secrets' of poetry, and are there exactly thirteen of them? Well, no; and as early as the second page Adrian Mitchell tells us that he's got twenty-one for us, as it happens – a characteristic piece of whimsy. The 'Thirteen Secrets' are a device, of course; a device not just to attract curiosity but one which also gives the book its structure.

Each 'secret' is revealed – or demonstrated – by a poem. These poems, taken together, comprise a small but very diverse collection: John Lennon rubs shoulders with WB Yeats, an Asian marketplace gives way to the Wild West, a sad voice from a block of flats is echoed by Tennyson's song about the owl. These poems are stitched together by Mitchell's rhyming introductions which, taken together, become a poem about writing poetry. There is a third level of text, too: Mitchell's left-hand page 'footers', which comment, instruct or simply enthuse.

Adrian Mitchell is a campaigner, and this is a book with a mission – to urge children to write for themselves. We think it is appropriate for teachers to collaborate with Mitchell (and ourselves) in trying to achieve that; this book is not merely a test of children's comprehension, it is meant to be a source of their inspiration. Mitchell's insistence is that children can write out of their own experiences, no matter how ordinary and simple these might seem, and should not be deterred by the cleverness of 'real' poetry. This is not a book that puts poetry on a pedestal.

Valerie Littlewood's illustrations have much of the same swirling energy and variety that the poems and Mitchell himself have, and they often insinuate little insights into the text.

You could take children through the whole collection sequentially. Or you could range freely, as we do – our suggestions for guided reading activities focus on certain of the poems and the connections between them, as well as Adrian Mitchell's 'Welcome' to the book and those 'Extra Secrets'.

About the author

Adrian Mitchell was born in London in 1932. He is a highly regarded, prolific and versatile writer. As well as numerous collections of poetry for both young and adult readers he has written plays, screenplays, novels, libretti, song lyrics, political pamphlets, journalistic pieces and essays. He is a William Blake enthusiast; he has inspired and supported writers such as Brian Pattern and Roger McGough; he is famed for his live readings. He can be dead serious, but his writing is usually infused with a wonderfully quirky, almost surrealist wit. He would not be insulted if you called him a romantic. All these elements in his work are perhaps summarised by the title of one of his collections: *Love Songs For World War Three.*

GUIDED READING NOTES

46

Begin by discussing the book's appearance. What do the front cover and title lead children to expect? Are they surprised to learn that poetry has secrets? Can they suggest what they might be? Now read the blurb on the back cover. What does it tell us? How much of it is a 'tease' and how much is information? Have the children read anything by Adrian Mitchell already? Is it a surprise to discover that this book is an anthology of poetry? Flick quickly through the book to demonstrate the way it is organised – Mitchell's 'secrets', his advice and comments on the left-hand pages and poems on the right.

Read with the group the double-page spread 'Welcome to the Thirteen Secrets'. From the very first sentence, we get a sense of Adrian Mitchell's personality through his tone of voice; he begins with a joke about his age. (How old was he really when he wrote this introduction? It can be worked out from the third paragraph.) How would the group describe this 'voice', this personality? How does he speak about poetry? Can the children summarise the feeling for poetry that comes across?

What is this piece of writing really about – reading poetry, or writing it? Ask the children to pick out the things that Mitchell says we need to write poetry (time, imagination and skill, paragraph 5) and the thing that all poems must have (rhythm, paragraph 8).

What do the children think of the ideas in this piece? Is the last paragraph meant to put them off writing poetry?

Read with the group Secret One and 'The Wildest Wheelbarrow'. Which paragraphs in 'Welcome to the Thirteen Secrets' do these texts relate to? (Paragraphs 7 and 8.)

Children might not know what Mitchell means by *outright rock 'n' roll*. He may have had Chuck Berry's 'Brown-Eyed Handsome Man' in mind; it would be good to listen to it. Try to read the poem aloud as rhythmically as possible. (Some references, for example *GBH*, *Robert de Niro*, *microfiche* may need explaining.)

Ask the children if they can spot familiar poetical 'tricks' used to add extra 'punch' to the beat, such as end-rhymes, variation in line length, and the alliterations of *w* falling on the stressed syllables at the ends of the first and third stanzas. Do *all* the lines fit the rhythm exactly? Are there any that are difficult to read? Ask the children to read aloud the last line of the second stanza, and then read it again without the word *eighty*. Which works best?

Is this a nonsense poem, like Lewis Carroll's 'Jabberwocky'? Why not? (Because although it's wild and fantastical, it consists of recognisable words – used in a very odd way, of course.)

Ask the children to read independently Secret Two and John Lennon's 'I Remember Arnold' and find the words that Lennon made up – what might they mean? Would other, real words have worked as well?

Read Secret Four and Yeats' 'The Lake Isle of Innisfree'.
Adrian Mitchell implies that Yeats' poem is a 'wish-list', but it's a great deal more than that, of course; it's a fantasy, a dream, a desire for peace, an image that gives the poet spiritual comfort, an escapist reverie.

Try to bring out the musicality of the language as you read it. Can the children identify some of the sound effects that give the poem that quality: those long and round vowels in words like *bean, bee, peace, go, glow, loud, made, glade, noon*; the long smooth lines; internal rhyme, the use of punctuation to slow the pace?

At first, the poem is very particular in its details: what the cabin will be made of, exactly how many bean-rows, and so on. But do the children

begin to suspect that this is not a real place, or that it is *more than* a real place? If so, when? At the end, where do we learn that the lapping of the lake water is in *the deep heart's core*? Or before that? When might we begin to suspect that the Isle is an idealised place? How does the dream-like, trance-like sound of the language help us to understand the meaning of the poem, and the meaning that the Lake Isle has for the poet?

Next read Secret Eleven and 'There Will Come Soft Rains' by Sara Teasdale. Because it's about something horrible, it ought perhaps to be very different to Yeats' lovely verse. But the first two rhyming couplets are actually rather similar to it; can the children identify some of the same sound effects?

How would they describe the word picture Teasdale is painting here? There's a sudden change in the poem at the fourth couplet; the word *war* comes as a complete surprise. Can the children identify how the language changes? All figurative, metaphorical language vanishes; this couplet and the next are flat, plain, bare.

Encourage the children to use the word *personification* to describe what happens in the last couplet.

This poem imagines the complete extinction of humankind after a world war. How, in books and movies, is such a world usually depicted? Isn't it a shock to find it depicted as beautiful instead? Can the children sympathise with the idea that people are not only destructive but actually unimportant?

Read Secret Seven and 'Listening' with the group.
Mitchell's tip here is about being prepared to jot things down, and it's good advice – most writers say that things they overhear by chance can provide a rich seam of ideas and dialogue.

His poem, though, is about sounds; and he does something very interesting with words – adjectives and nouns, in particular. Ask the children to pick out the words used as adjectives, and to identify the nouns they apply to. Do they notice anything strange? Take *glistening*, for example: the subject is snails, so the word we might expect after *glistening* is *trail*, but we get *song*. Or take *silver* in the last line, used to describe not a unicorn's horn, but its *hoofsteps*. What's going on? In these two examples, Mitchell is transferring a word belonging to one sense – sight – to another sense,

CONT. . .

47

SCHOLASTIC LITERACY CENTRES

CONT. . .

hearing. (There's an interesting word for this device, which word magpies in your class might like: *synaesthesia*, or 'sense-mixing'.) This a very useful device for writers because the vocabulary available for describing sound is much smaller than the vocabulary for describing sight; so this transferring across senses gives Mitchell a lot more choice. The phrase *stormy tree* is another instance of using an 'inappropriate' adjective; trees can't be stormy, strictly speaking, but the phrase conjures up perfectly the image Mitchell wants to get across. What these images do is create slightly baffling new ideas. They do what good poetry often does – *surprise* us, and make us look at things with new eyes.

Ask the children to read independently Secrets Nine and Twelve; in different ways they suggest being more aware of all our senses when we write. Do the children think that climbing a tree might provide a good source of words to describe a tree? How can we write about taste? (Raw fish might not inspire all the children, though!)

Read Secret Eight and 'Pleasant Sounds' by John Clare. Remind the children that rhyme is not a matter of spelling, it's a matter of *sound*, and that rhymes are a kind of echo that can occur within lines as well as at the ends of lines. Yet most of us expect poetry to end-rhyme, because it's enjoyable to predict what's coming next. Can the children see the joke in Mitchell's lines on the left-hand page?

Clare's wonderful poem doesn't have end-rhyme, but it has all sorts of other sound effects. Can the children spot them? Can they find examples of assonance – the repeating of vowel sounds (for example,

leaves/feet), consonance – the repeating of consonants (for example, *whizzing/ buzzards*), alliteration (for example, *wood/while/wind*)? Clare's delightful enthusiasm for natural sounds is too great to be imprisoned by the demands of conventional rhyme schemes, but he has a great ear for the music of words. Children should be encouraged by that.

Ask the children to read Tennyson's 'The Owl' (attached to Secret Six). This is another 'nature poem', but one that *does* have a strict pattern of rhyme and repetition. Which of the two do the children prefer? Do they feel 'safer' with the more conventional, rhyming poem?

Finally, read 'Extra Secrets' on the last page. By now, the children will have twigged that the word *secrets* is a tease. They may be able to use the word *ironic* to describe the way Mitchell uses it, since he is actually saying that although writing poetry takes skill it is something we all have within us, something we can all do if we want to. Are there any rhyming secrets on this page that children would challenge? (How about 21, for example? Isn't it a 'rule' that a sonnet has 14 lines? Would it be more true to say that poetry does have rules but no one makes you keep to them?) Do these secrets – along with those in the body of the book – encourage children to write? In short, has the book worked?

ACTIVITY NOTES

Spell to Banish a Pimple

Objective: to annotate a poem in preparation for a performance reading.
Resources: photocopiable page 55, writing materials.
Activity: Read aloud the poem 'Spell to Banish a Pimple' on the photocopiable sheet. Read it in a flat way without any preparation – it won't sound very interesting. Discuss with the children the ways in which a spell *ought* to be uttered. Point out to them that the poem is unpunctuated, so it is up to them to decide where pauses and stresses should fall.

Ask the children to annotate the poem to help them read it aloud or perform it, as a group. Is the group going to divide into parts, or read the poem 'ensemble'? Remind them to think about the sort of voice they will use, whether it will be loud or soft, fast or slow. Is there a pause at the end of each line? If not, where will the pauses be? Annotations might be: pencil lines connecting lines of the poem which should be run together; strokes for pauses (double and treble strokes for longer pauses); underlines for emphases; 'stage directions' (for example, *whispering*, *outraged*, *pointing*). However, children might want to devise their own annotation systems – using coloured highlighters, perhaps.

Finally, ask the children to think about whether they would want props to perform with – red lipstick to make a pimple? A mirror (or just a frame) to talk to?
Extension: The ballad 'Jesse James' (Secret Ten) readily lends itself to performance and choral reading. Ask the children to annotate it as above, and to 'script' it for single voices and choruses.

Magic poem

Objective: to model writing on an existing form.
Resources: copies of *The Thirteen Secrets of Poetry*, paper, writing materials.
Activity: This relates Secret Six *(Be happy to copy)* to Secret Three *(Write your poems/For a real reason)*. Revisit Secret Three and suggest that children write their own 'spell' or 'charm', using John Agard's poem as a model. Encourage them to write in rhythmic lines that could be chanted. Rhymes would be helpful, but children shouldn't let themselves get stuck trying to think of them.

Their spells could be to banish things such as curls from their hair, Brussels sprouts, spiders in the bath, brothers. A spell to banish a wart might begin:

Wart on my thumb, wart on my thumb
Where'd you come frumb?

And spells can be used to conjure up things: perhaps pizza and ice cream for school dinner, snow, a win for Aston Villa, two birthdays a year, teeth without braces.
Extension: Children could annotate their own poems for performance, as in the previous activity.

An inner world

Objective: to use both theme and structure of an existing poem to achieve new writing.
Resources: photocopiable page 56, copies of *The Thirteen Secrets of Poetry*, writing materials.
Activity: Read or revisit WB Yeats' 'The Lake Isle of Innisfree' (Secret Four) and remind the children that it describes a place that exists in the poet's mind as an 'inner world', a place apart from the fretful business of the real world. Do the children have their own 'Innisfrees'? If they had dream worlds they could escape to, what would they be like? Would they seek peace or excitement, company or solitude? Would they prefer a warm desert island or a winter wonderland? Ask the children to devise their 'inner worlds', using the photocopiable sheet as a template. Challenge them, in completing the first part of the activity, to get as close to the form of Yeats' poem as they can. For the second part, they should write in any form they like. (If they have trouble getting started, there are ideas provided on the sheet.)

Jenny

Objective: to write imaginatively about a character from a poem, drawing on details from the text.
Resources: copies of *The Thirteen Secrets of Poetry*, paper, writing materials.
Activity: This is a writing activity to be undertaken individually. Begin by reading or re-reading 'Double Glazing' by Brian Patten (Secret Five). Ask the children to build on the details in the poem to imagine Jenny and her life. They might want to think about questions such as: how old is Jenny? What does she look like? What is the flat she lives in like? What happens on her estate? How does she spend the time when she's not at school? Ask the children to write a short piece about Jenny *either* in the first person as a diary entry *or* as a poem written in the third person beginning with the words *Jenny wakes...*

The colour of sound

Objectives: to understand the way a writer achieves particular effects; to experiment with sensory metaphors; to use these experiments to inform personal writing.
Resources: photocopiable page 57, copies of *The Thirteen Secrets of Poetry*, a dice for each pair of children, paper, writing materials.
Activity: This is a 'sense-mixing' activity for children working in pairs. Begin by briefly revisiting Adrian Mitchell's 'Listening' (Secret Seven) and reminding the children of the way the poet creates interesting ideas by 'confusing' vision and sound as in *silver hoofsteps*. This is actually a rather difficult thing to do consciously; the photocopiable sheet allows children to do it randomly. There are two pairs of lists, A and B, and C and D. One child rolls the dice to select an adjective from list A, then writes it down. His or her partner then does likewise to select a phrase from list B, and adds it to the adjective; thus a 6 and a 2 gets *The misty sigh of the sea*, for example. Repeat the process for lists C and D.

When the children have compiled 12 combinations from each list, they should select those they think are the most interesting and use them to write a 'list' poem like Mitchell's, or a form of their own devising.

Extension: Alter the activity, so that children:
■ compile phrases, combining words from lists A and D, and C and B
■ roll dice to apply *two* adjectives to each phrase
■ select a second adjective of their own choice, thus consciously working towards a particular idea.

Juggling with jottings

Objective: to write poems based on the senses, using children's notes of their own experiences.

Resources: photocopiable page 58, copies of *The Thirteen Secrets of Poetry*, paper, writing materials.

Activity: This is a development from the previous activity: instead of experimenting with received words and phrases, children evolve their own. Briefly revisit Secret Nine, in which Mitchell suggests that the way we experience things with *all* our senses can be used to help us write.

Ask the children to fill in the three boxes on the photocopiable sheet labelled *Sight*, *Sound* and *Feel* with adjectives from these three senses (for example, *sparkling*, *piercing*, *greasy*). Encourage them to try to think of some unusual and interesting adjectives.

Next, ask them to jot down, on the 'notebook' section of the sheet, details of an out-of-school activity they remember enjoying recently, such as a good game of football, going somewhere with a friend. (You might ask for this to be done over a weekend.)

Finally, ask the children to apply these adjectives to their notebook jottings in imaginative ways to form interesting phrases to build into short poems.

I hear

Objectives: to understand the significance of expressive verb forms; to compile and use expressive verb forms.

Resources: photocopiable page 59, copies of *The Thirteen Secrets of Poetry*, writing materials, thesauruses (optional).

Activity: Briefly revisit John Clare's 'Pleasant Sounds' (Secret Eight) and look at his use of verbal nouns – that is, verbs used as nouns, as in *The rustling, The whizzing, the pattering*. The activity on the photocopiable sheet challenges children to think of (or even invent) verbal nouns for different sources of sound. Ask the children to try to fill the boxes, then form their chosen words into sentences and arrange them into a short poem (or use them as lines in a longer poem) called simply 'I Hear'.

Would the real Jesse James please stand up

Objectives: to encourage close reading of a text based on real characters and incidents; to use research to check the text's presentation of facts.

Resources: copies of *The Thirteen Secrets of Poetry*, print and ICT reference sources, writing materials.

Activity: Ask the children to read 'Jesse James' (Secret Ten). You could then read it aloud to them. Encourage them to think about the anonymous author's attitude

51

SCHOLASTIC LITERACY CENTRES

towards his subject. Does the writer justify calling Ford a *dirty little coward*? Why might the writer – and other *people* – have admired the James Gang, if they were criminals? Was Jesse perhaps a bit like Robin Hood? Who might Captain Sheets and *the agent* have been?

After discussing the poem, provide the children with reference books to research Jesse James and the James Gang (they could also search the Internet, where they will find plenty of material). They should make notes, working independently or in pairs.

Do all the facts the children gather tally with the ballad version? How much of the poem might be 'poetic licence' or invention – for example, how could the first line be verified?

Extension: Ask the children to use incidents or characters they discover in their research to write extra verses, trying to keep to the rough ballad form of the original by counting the 'beats' per line (which is more important than rhyme).

A hate plate

Objective: to invent metaphors and use them to express a personal feeling or experience.

Resources: photocopiable page 60, copies of *The Thirteen Secrets of Poetry*, writing materials.

Activity: Ask the children to read Secret Eleven and Sara Teasdale's 'There Will Come Soft Rains'. Ask them to think of a thing, a feeling or an experience that they hate and to write it on the 'hate plate' on the photocopiable sheet. (Children might work in pairs if they share a pet hate.) Then they should try to fill the boxes with nouns, verbs and adjectives they associate with the word(s) on the plate; this vocabulary should help them to invent similes.

Finally, the children should try to compose a 'definition poem', using metaphors. A 'definition poem' is one which gets its form by repeating the key word and offering different 'definitions': *Fear is... Fear is...* and so on. Remind the children that the simplest way of turning a simile into a metaphor is to leave out the word *like*. *Fear is a spider sitting on my neck* (metaphor) is somehow stronger than *Fear is like a spider sitting on my neck* (simile).

Freeze-frames

Objective: to focus on the immediate environment and write about it in a fresh way.

Resources: photocopiable page 61, copies of *The Thirteen Secrets of Poetry*, clipboards, writing materials, some cardboard tubes or small, open-ended boxes to use as 'viewfinders', dry weather.

Activity: In Secret Twelve Adrian Mitchell describes daydreaming as being in charge of a camera filming the movies inside one's head. This activity – for pairs of children – uses the idea of a camera viewfinder to enable them to look at details of their surroundings in a new way by separating these details from their contexts. These contexts might be the classroom, the school's garden or wild area, the playground – whatever you think is appropriate.

Ask the children to imagine the cardboard tube or box as a camera. One of each pair should 'track' it until he or she fixes on an interesting detail. The 'cameraman' should then dictate to his or her partner what is inside the 'frame'. It is important that he or she doesn't *name* what's in the frame, but *describes* it. So, for example, it is not *the corner of the goal*, it's *metal turning a corner in front of a net*. Ask the children to write their notes in the appropriate places of the photocopiable sheet.

The children should change roles twice. When each pair has four 'shots' they should polish and sequence them to read to the rest of the class as poems. The other children should try to guess what is being described and where the readers have been – a form of riddling.

Extension: Riddles are a good device for writing about familiar things in an interesting way. Challenge children to write detailed descriptions of things and their functions without naming them, and present them to the class to solve.

Baby talk, baby talk back

Objective: to write in two 'voices'.

Resources: copies of *The Thirteen Secrets of Poetry*, paper, writing materials.

Activity: Read or revisit 'Poem to be Played with a Baby' (Secret Thirteen) as a preliminary to this work. All the children will have been subjected to 'baby talk' – nonsense words, sounds, toe- and finger-counting rhymes, bouncing rhymes and so on that adults use to communicate with babies.

Ask the children if they can remember any baby talk – they might have heard it at home, if they have younger siblings, or snippets of it at the school gate. Can they write it down? Perhaps they could collect examples over a few days or the weekend (by asking their mums and dads what they used to say, if they have no new parents to eavesdrop on). They will need to be phonetically inventive: is *Oochee-koochee-koo* the correct spelling, for example?

When the group has a good-sized compilation, ask them to imagine what a baby might think or say in response if he or she had the vocabulary of a ten- or eleven-year-old. Ask the children to write, using, if appropriate, the sort of 'stage directions' that Mitchell uses, a dialogue between an adult and a baby. Have a laugh.

Shuffling the secrets

Objective: to review and evaluate Adrian Mitchell's poetry-writing tips.

Resources: photocopiable page 62, copies of *The Thirteen Secrets of Poetry*, A3 paper, scissors, glue, drawing and colouring materials.

Activity: The photocopiable sheet runs together the texts in the 'secrets' panels, separated by cutting lines. The texts are set out in the sequence in which they appear in the book and make a sort of poem, but is this the best or only possible sequence? Or the best or only poem? Ask the children to separate them by cutting along the lines, and then to try ordering them in different sequences until they find one they like best.

Several criteria are possible. Sound patterns is one; children might notice that they get a six-line mini-poem, with four consecutive lines rhyming, by running texts 5 and 2 together. Or they might try for a 'logical' progression, starting with text 9 and following it with text 7. When the children are satisfied with their re-sequencing, ask them to glue their 'new poems' onto sheets of A3 paper. They can then illustrate their texts with their own images.

Picture this

Objective: to assess the contribution to an anthology made by its illustrator.

Resources: copies of *The Thirteen Secrets of Poetry*, paper, writing materials. For the extension – art materials.

Activity: Begin by asking the children to look again at Valerie Littlewood's illustrations of the poems in the anthology. You may need to point out that some of her illustrations are inspired by a single image taken from a poem (for example, the mermaid illustrating Sujata Bhatt's poem, Secret Nine), while others try to reflect the whole thing ('Double Glazing', Secret Five; 'Jesse James', Secret Ten); and that her illustrations vary greatly in mood and style.

Ask the children if there is an illustration they like best, and to write explanations for their choices. Suggest *mood, colour, style, appropriateness* as guideline headings. The children should try to explain how their chosen illustration adds to the poem and helps the reader to appreciate it.

Extension: Ask the children to select an illustration they don't much like or think they could improve; how would they do better? Let them try out their ideas.

My secret page

Objective: to compile a class/group anthology, using the format of *The Thirteen Secrets of Poetry*.

Resources: photocopiable page 63 (enlarged, if necessary), copies of *The Thirteen Secrets of Poetry*, other poetry collections, writing and drawing materials.

Activity: Ask the children to decide which secret or tip for writing poetry they think is the best. It may be one of the thirteen secrets or one of the extra secrets from the final page of the book. Better still, they may be able to devise a 'secret' of their own.

Challenge the children to devise their own 'secret' pages, using the photocopiable sheet, which is based on the format of a double-page spread from *The Thirteen Secrets of Poetry*. (Using the template should help the children by giving them a structure for their work and by giving a consistent appearance to their end-product.) Encourage them to write their secret in verse at the top of the left-hand page and to explain it in more detail at the bottom of the page. To complete the layout they need to choose a poem that exemplifies their secret and to copy it out (or part of it) and illustrate it.

Name   Date

Spell to Banish a Pimple

Get back pimple

get back to where you belong

Get back to never-never land

and I hope you stay there long

Get back pimple

get back to where you belong

How dare you take up residence

in the middle of my face

I never offered you a place

beside my dimple

Get back pimple

get back to where you belong

Get packing pimple

I banish you to outer space

If only life was that simple

John Agard

Name _____   Date _____

An inner world

Do you have an inner world of your own, like Yeats' 'The Lake Isle of Innisfree' – a place you can escape to in your daydreams? What is its name? What sort of a place is it? What would you build there?

❏ Write four lines of a poem about your inner world, using the beginning of Yeats' poem as a model:

I will arise and go now, and go to

_____

And a _____ build there,

of _____

_____

❏ Write four lines about your fantasy world in any form you like:

_____

_____

_____

_____

castle, ice rink, theme park, space cruiser, cyber heaven, Hollywood, underwater world, coral cave, palace, the kingdom of chocolate, pool, beach house, the deep green forest, roller-coaster, winter wonderland, tree house, film set, Old Trafford, milkshake, desert island, villa

Name _____   Date _____

The colour of sound

Use a dice to invent weird and wonderful phrases! Roll the dice to pick a word from list A, then roll it again to pick a phrase from list B. Combine them on a separate piece of paper. So, if you throw a 1 and then a 3, you write **The shadowy voices of children**. Take turns with your partner to roll the dice. When you've got 12 combinations, do the same with lists C and D.

From your 24 combinations, pick the six you think are the most interesting. Could this list become a poem?

A	The		B	
	1. shadowy			1. call of an owl
	2. symmetrical			2. sigh of the sea
	3. blue			3. voices of children
	4. cracked			4. purring of a cat
	5. glittering			5. beat of a drum
	6. misty			6. ticking of a clock

C	The		D	
	1. dazzling			1. taste of chocolate
	2. green			2. fizz of lemonade
	3. round			3. wind in the trees
	4. glossy			4. whoosh of a firework
	5. pale			5. scent of a white rose
	6. transparent			6. flavour of onions

Our 6 most interesting combinations are:

1. _____

2. _____

3. _____

4. _____

5. _____

6. _____

■SCHOLASTIC

57

SCHOLASTIC LITERACY CENTRES

Name _____   Date _____

Juggling with jottings

Fill the three boxes with as many adjectives to do with these three senses as you can think of. There's one in each to start you off. Try to think of interesting and unusual ones.

Sight	Sound	Feel
dazzling	shrill	gritty

Next, jot down in this notebook notes about something interesting you've done recently: a visit somewhere, a game of football, even being ill.

Now, on another sheet of paper, turn your notes into a story or a poem. Mix into it adjectives from your boxes to make new and interesting phrases. How many adjectives can you fit in? What's the strangest phrase you invent?

Name

Date

I hear

In John Clare's poem 'Pleasant Sounds', the poet uses verbal nouns such as **the rustling, the whizzing**. Think of good verbal nouns to go in the first set of boxes. Try to hear these sounds in your head. In the second set of boxes, write things the verbal nouns might apply to.

1. The	of a dog's claws on a hard floor
2. The	of water in a drainpipe
3. The	of a child eating spaghetti
4. The	of cars driving through puddles
5. The	of my own heart
6. The	of insects in the long grass
7. The	of an old man snoring

A. The sighing	of
B. The whirring	of
C. The giggling	of
D. The crunching	of
E. The howling	of

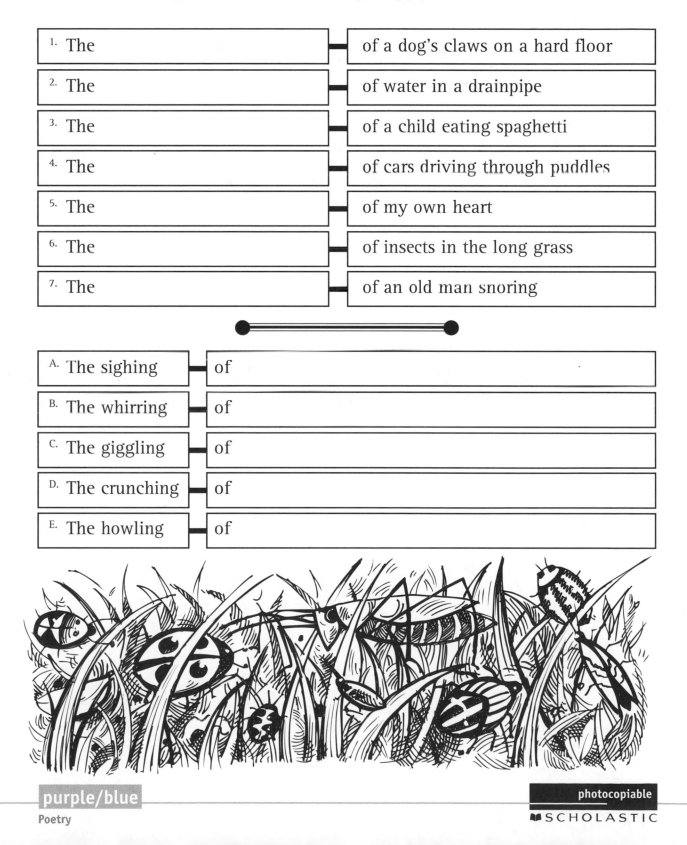

SCHOLASTIC LITERACY CENTRES

Name   Date

A hate plate

Do you have a pet hate? Write it on the 'hate plate'. Fill the boxes with verbs, nouns and adjectives connected with what's on the hate plate. Then invent similes using some of the words you've thought of, for example **Anger is like a red alligator**.

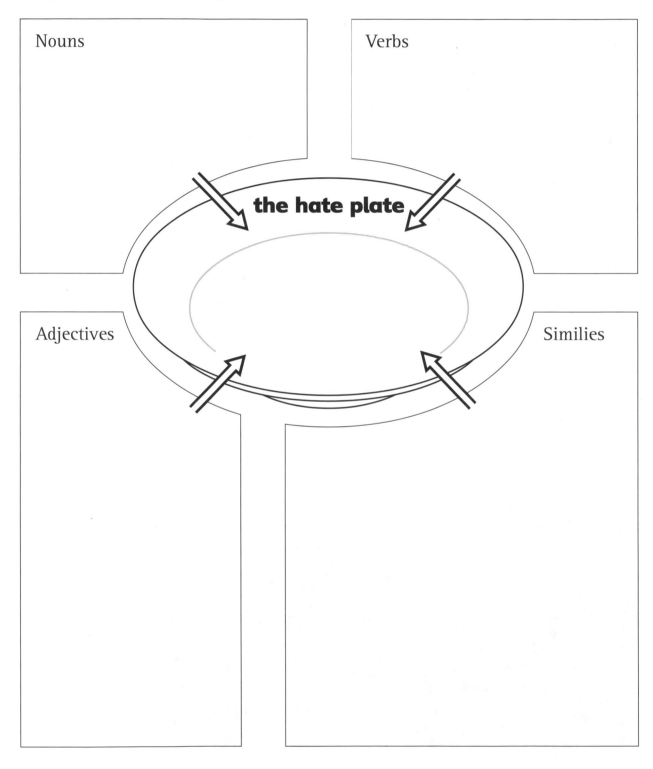

Name _____   Date _____

Freeze-frames

In the freeze-frames, write what your partner sees through the view-finder. Remember that the words should describe what can be **seen**, but mustn't **name** it. When you've done **two** frames each, write them out as little stanzas. (You can add new words if you think of any.) Read your poem to the class: can they guess where you've been and what you've seen?

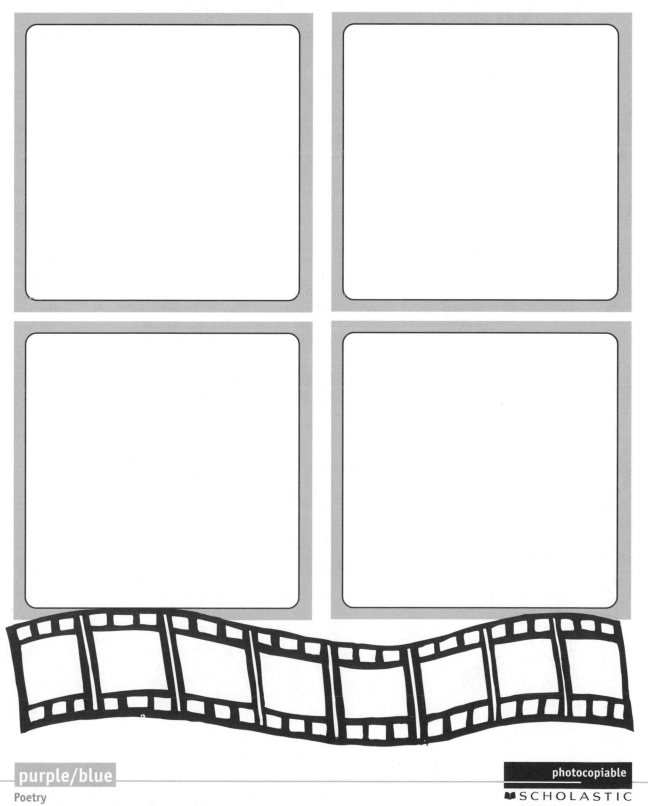

SCHOLASTIC LITERACY CENTRES

Name   Date

Shuffling the secrets

> Use your feet
> To find the beat.

> If the old word won't do
> Make up a new.

> Don't write about Autumn
> Because that's the season –
> Write your poems
> For a real reason.

> Write to cool down
> Write to get hot
> Write about things
> You like a lot.

> Write for other people;
> Quite a few
> Will sit down and write
> A poem for you.

> Like a poppy-field poppy
> Be happy to copy.

> Good ideas often fly off and so
> Take that notebook wherever you go
> (and three pens).

> You can rhyme every time at the end of a line
> And that's no crime if the words feel fine,
> But on the other hand you can write a poem
> Which doesn't have any rhymes at all.

> What can you write about?
> It helps very much
> If you choose something
> You can see and touch.

> Maybe the search for food
> Maybe a quest for glory,
> But write a poem
> With a story.

> Pile up your feelings
> On a poetry plate –
> Write about something
> You really hate.

> To make a poem
> That lasts a minute
> Daydream for hours
> Before you begin it.

> Don't just write
> For the literate few –
> Write for babies
> And animals too.

Name   Date

My secret page

SCHOLASTIC LITERACY CENTRES

My Last Nature Walk

Background

In Lewis Carroll's *Through the Looking Glass*, Humpty Dumpty 'explains' the poem 'Jabberwocky' to Alice; in 'My Last Nature Walk' Adrian Mitchell provides a glossary to his own poem. In both cases, the result is even greater mystification. Being happily baffled is the chief pleasure of nonsense verse which, importantly, encourages us to enjoy the sound of words unhindered by their meaning. All the same, we somehow can't help trying to work out what a nonsense poem might mean in 'ordinary' words. It's our desire to 'translate' that Adrian Mitchell makes fun of; this teasing, but with a serious purpose, is typical of him, as children familiar with *The Thirteen Secrets of Poetry* will know. In this extra text poem, there is also an element of parody.

■ Read the first four lines of William Wordsworth's 'Daffodils' to the children (see below), then read the first four lines of 'My Last Nature Walk' on photocopiable page 66 and invite comparisons between the two.

> *I wander'd lonely as a cloud*
> *That floats on high o'er vales and hills,*
> *When all at once I saw a crowd,*
> *A host of golden daffodils.*

Encourage the children to see that the first lines are very similar in form. Adrian Mitchell's lines are a *parody* of Wordsworth's. 'Daffodils' is probably the best-known 'nature poem' in English. It is as if Mitchell is saying, 'Right – this is a nature poem, so I'd better make it sound like Wordsworth'.

■ Now read the whole of Mitchell's poem. Although it makes a serious point about our need to make sense of, or 'translate', the world around us, it should be fun to read and work with. Which poem in *The Thirteen Secrets of Poetry* does it most resemble? (John Lennon's 'I Remember Arnold'.) Which is the more nonsensical, and why? In which poem is it easier to 'guess the meaning' of invented words from their contexts? What kind of story is this poem pretending to tell? What usually has a moral? (A fable.)

■ Without consulting the glossary, is it possible to say anything about the meanings of these invented words from their context? Can the children use the phrase *parts of speech* in answering this question? What parts of speech might *gollamonce* and *glumped* be, and how can we tell they are not the same? Can children classify other nonsense words in terms of grammatical function?

■ What observations about the glossary can the children make? Can they see that it is progressively less helpful? The definition of *clumihacken* is just about feasible, and *whump* does sound rather like what Mitchell says it means. How do these definitions differ from that of *groolted*? Do the children know the word *paradox*, and see one in the definitions of *balore*, *gurch* and *gollamonce*? Why are the last two definitions absolutely unhelpful? Which two words are not in the glossary? (*Laughter-rafter* and *after-laughter-rafter*.) What's the joke, here? There are two, really. One is the joke played on the reader – we spend all this time working this stuff out and end up none the wiser. The other is a more serious joke at the expense of people who think that the meaning of a poem can be worked out by 'translating' it into other words.

■ Photocopiable page 67 offers the chance to invent new definitions for Mitchell's glossary; ask the children to keep parts of speech in mind.

■ Ask the children what goes through their minds when they try to 'translate' nonsense words. Do they look for similarities to other words, or a common word root? Is there something in the sound of the word which suggests a meaning? Use photocopiable page 68 to explore these questions. Again, remind the children to decide which part of speech they are looking for.

■ Although its language is impenetrable, the poem is conventional in other ways. Can the children say how? (It is regular in both rhyme and rhythm, as they should have noticed when they compared it with Wordsworth's 'Daffodils'.) Photocopiable page 69 is a cloze of Walter De La Mare's 'Silver'. Ask the children to fill the gaps with nonsense words of their own, trying to keep a steady rhythm and maintaining rhyme.

■ Finally, can the children suggest what Mitchell is doing in this poem (apart from enjoying himself, of course)? Why provide a 'meaningless' glossary? Is he perhaps saying that we shouldn't go looking for ordinary meanings when we read nonsense verse? Come to that, why do poets write nonsense verse in the first place, and why does it remain popular?

assessment

ASSESSMENT NOTES

Six secrets

Assessment focus: to recall some of Adrian Mitchell's 'secrets' for writing poetry.
Resources: photocopiable page 70, writing materials.
Activity: The children should attempt this activity individually and without reference to the book, which means that accurate rephrasing is fine, if verbatim recall fails them. Encourage the children to go beyond the bare bones; they should show an understanding of each secret by writing, for example: *It's fine to copy other poets because...*

A radio review

Assessment focus: to review a book according to given criteria; to express a critical opinion.
Resources: photocopiable page 71, copies of *The Thirteen Secrets of Poetry*, paper, writing materials.
Activity: Ask the children to prepare a short talk in the form of a review of *The Thirteen Secrets of Poetry* for a radio programme. The photocopiable sheet offers a 'flow diagram' method of organising the review. Remind the children to use note form on the sheet; complete sentences are part of the second half of the activity. Children are likely to be surprised by how many words it takes to occupy a one-minute talk.
Extension: Suggest that the children research biographical information about Adrian Mitchell. They should arrange it in a way that makes it easy to read aloud, and add it to the review.

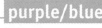

My Last Nature Walk

I strode among the clumihacken
Where scrubble nudges to the barfter
Till I whumped into, hidden in the bracken,
A groolted after-laughter-rafter.

(For milty Wah-Zohs do guffaw
Upon a laughter-rafter perch.
But after laughter they balore
Unto a second beam to gurch.)
Yet here was but one gollamonce!
I glumped upon the after-laughter-rafter.
Where was its other-brother? Oh! My bonce!
The Wah-Zohs blammed it with a laughter-rafter.

Moral: Never gamble on a bramble ramble.

Glossary:
clumihacken – the old stalks of wild Brussels sprouts
scrubble – unusually tall moss, often scuffed
the barfter – the height at which low clouds cruise
to whump – to bump into, winding oneself in the process
groolted – cunningly engraved with the portraits of
    little-known and famous barbers
milty – clean but mean-minded
Wah-Zohs – French birds, sometimes spelt Oiseaux
to balore – to hover fatly downwards
to gurch – to recover from cheerfulness
gollamonce – a thing that is sought for desperately,
    although there is no good reason for finding it
to glump – to glump
to blam – to shonk on the cloddle

Adrian Mitchell

A gormless glossary

Prove you can be nuttier than Adrian Mitchell! Here are the words from the glossary to 'My Last Nature Walk'. See if you can come up with even dafter definitions – but think about which **part of speech** you're teasingly translating.

clumihacken _____

_____

scrubble _____

_____

the barfter _____

_____

to whump _____

_____

groolted _____

_____

milty _____

_____

Wah-Zohs _____

_____

to balore _____

_____

to gurch _____

_____

gollamonce _____

_____

to glump _____

_____

to blam _____

_____

Name _____   Date _____

Pure nonsense

Here are some more words for you to daftly define – which parts of speech
are they?

pipswitch _____

shiftingle _____

duggle _____

craspous _____

whirpy _____

grongerly _____

quelldoozled _____

snig _____

enscuffulate _____

unscumble _____

And here are some definitions for you to invent words for:

1. the fluff you find under your big toenail _____

2. a damp box to keep worms in _____

3. to have a dream that belongs to somebody else _____

4. to sing and laugh at the same time _____

5. a tree that eats chickens _____

6. a hammer made of glass _____

7. covered in soft spikes _____

8. to sneeze under water _____

9. a machine that squirts the jam into doughnuts _____

10. a game played with two bats, a net and a jelly _____

Name _____   Date _____

This poem is called...

Some of the words of this poem have been removed or changed because they were far too sensible. Replace them with words you have invented. One has been done for you. Can you keep a rhythm going? Can you make the lines rhyme? When you've filled the gaps, think of a title.

Title: _____

Slowly, _____, now the ___*gloon*_____

_____ the night in his _____ _____;

This way, and that, he _____, and sees

_____ fruit on _____ _____;

One by one the _____ catch

His _____ beneath the silvery _____;

_____ in his kennel, like a _____,

With _____ of silver sleeps the dog;

From their shadowy _____ the _____ _____ peep

Of _____ in silver-_____ _____;

A _____ _____ goes scampering by,

With _____ claws and _____ _____;

And _____ fish in the _____ gleam,

By _____ reeds in a _____ _____.

Name   Date

Six secrets

Some of Adrian Mitchell's 'secrets' of poetry are tips about getting ideas for a poem, others are about ways of using language. How many can you remember? Write one 'secret' in each of the boxes below. It doesn't matter if you can't remember the way Mitchell writes them – use your own words.

A secret about getting ideas	A secret about rhythm

A secret about imagining	A secret about words

A secret about rhyme	A secret about using other poems

photocopiable

SCHOLASTIC

Name   Date

A radio review

Michael Rosen presents a radio programme called *Treasure Islands*, which is all about books for children. Imagine that he has asked you to come on the show and review *The Thirteen Secrets of Poetry*. You have to speak about the book for up to a minute, no longer. Use this planner to make notes for your review; then write it and time how long it takes you to read it out.

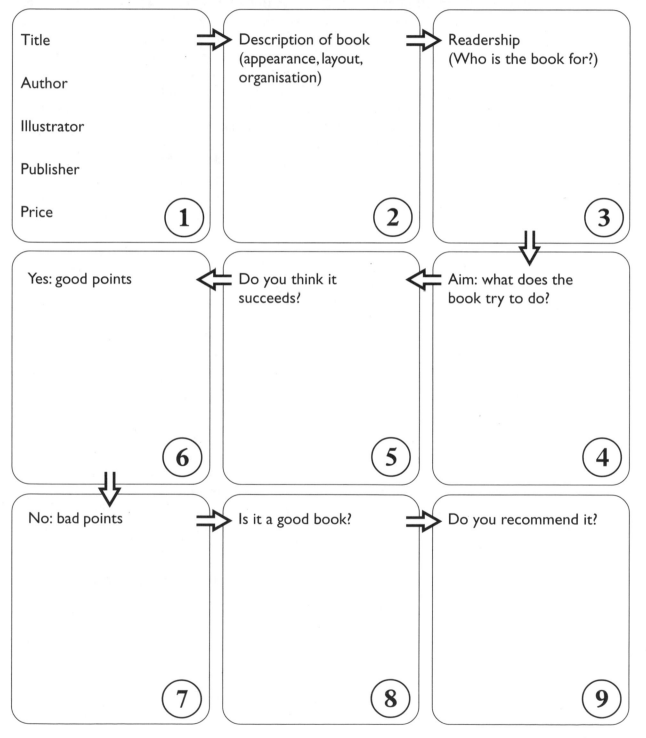

Title	Description of book (appearance, layout, organisation)	Readership (Who is the book for?)
Author		
Illustrator		
Publisher		
Price **①**	**②**	**③**
Yes: good points	Do you think it succeeds?	Aim: what does the book try to do?
⑥	**⑤**	**④**
No: bad points	Is it a good book?	Do you recommend it?
⑦	**⑧**	**⑨**

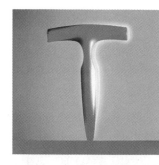

ALKING TURKEYS

BY BENJAMIN ZEPHANIAH

About the book

Benjamin Zephaniah is, above all, a voice. He is a performance poet, and his readings are wonderfully entertaining. *Talking Turkeys* (his first collection for children) conveys much of his spirit and many of his themes. *Even when I'm putting together poems for my books I can hear the music,* he has said; and in this book we can hear his love of rhythm and his pleasure in playing with words. His themes, such as a hatred of cruelty, sympathy with animals (and thus a campaigning veganism), a yearning for peaceful coexistence, and the all-inclusiveness of the English language, are all here.

Because Zephaniah is essentially a performer, his work can lose some impact on the printed page. (He has said that he prefers hearing poetry to reading it.) Little jokey rhymes delightfully thrown away on the stage can lose their sparkle in cold print. But, very interestingly, this book tries to reproduce some of the energy and unpredictability of a live performance through the techniques of typography and page design. This gives opportunities for you to consider how the *appearance* of a poem, and its relationship to illustration, can influence the way it is read. This book is as least as visual as it is literary.

When it comes to reading aloud many of Benjamin Zephaniah's poems, there is the problem of either having to 'Anglicise' the texts, or run the risk of ineptly parodying Anglo-Caribbean speech. Neither option is really acceptable. It would be best to admit to this difficulty, and share it with your class; a recording of the poet reading his work to acquaint children with the roles that accent, dialect, rhythm and music play in his poetry is advisable. It would also be a very good idea to collect tapes of accessible, well-written rap lyrics and play them as a preamble and background to reading the book.

About the author

Although Benjamin Zephaniah grew up in Birmingham, England, he was born in Jamaica and is proud of and inspired by his Jamaican ancestry; the sounds, colours and flavours of the Caribbean are essential to his writing. In his youth, he got on the wrong side of the law and was in prison for a spell, but he has said that it was in prison that he came to understand the power of language. For Zephaniah, music, singing and performing poetry live preceded writing poetry for print. He has made a number of albums, and has recorded with reggae legends Sly and Robbie; Bob Marley remains one of his heroes.

Benjamin Zephaniah is rightly celebrated as a performer, a comic poet and a children's poet, but even in these roles he always has an ideological and anti-racist edge; and his adult poetry has a lot of fire in its belly. He is energetically involved in campaigning for international human rights; Nelson Mandela is among his friends and admirers.

GUIDED READING NOTES

This is not a typical book of poetry. Explain that Zephaniah is a performance poet, and ask the children why putting performance poems into print might pose problems. What can a poet do 'live' that he cannot do in print? Can the group make the connection between performance and the appearance of the poems? How would they describe the pictures used in the book? Ask the children to look at the typography. Ask them to pick out different ways in which the text is printed. Finally, look at the language of the poems. Explain to the children that these poems use dialect and that the way the dialect words are spelled allows the reader to 'hear' the voice of the poet.

Ask the children to bear these features – illustration, typography and dialect – in mind as they read 'De Generation Rap' (pages 44–5), 'Beyond De Bell' (pages 56–7), 'Sunnyside Up' (page 92) and 'According to My Mood' (pages 24–5). Share with the children the linguistic and typographical jokes in 'According to My Mood' that 'act out' the ideas in the poem.

Zephaniah frequently uses repeated words and phrases to create the rhythms in his poems. Can the children skim through the book and find poems in which a particular word or phrase is repeated? Examples include 'A Day in the Life of Danny the Cat' (pages 36–9), 'Rap Connected' (pages 50–1), 'Body Talk' (pages 14–15) and 'Movie Madness' (pages 78–9).

In 'Rap Connected', Zephaniah uses the repeated phrase *We were born to*... as a sort of challenge. Take this repeated phrase and ask the children to think of their own continuation of the line before reading the poem. (See also the activity 'Connected' below.) Read aloud 'Body Talk' to show how Zephaniah repeats *Dere's* and *In me* to create the poem's rap rhythm (but note how he varies and departs from these phrases to create change and surprise).

Zephaniah uses repetition for a different purpose in 'Running' (pages 16–17) and 'De Generation Rap' (pages 44–5). Here, the repetition gives the poem a theme: to exhaust all the ways of using the word *run* in 'Running' and to give all the cool terminology we could apply to a 'he' or 'she' in 'De Generation Rap'.

Zephaniah's poetry explores a range of controversial issues. Explain to the children that, as they read such poetry, they will have the dual task of understanding the poem's viewpoint and thinking through their own response. Point them towards five particular poems: 'Royal Tea' (pages 26–7), 'A Killer Lies' (pages 52–3), 'Civil Lies' (pages 58–9), 'Memories' (pages 68–9) and 'I' (page 74). Zephaniah is looking at royalty, blood sports, the Eurocentric view of history, veganism and sexism. What standpoints does he take on the issues he explores and how do the children respond to them? For example, can they state Zephaniah's viewpoint in 'Civil Lies' as a prose sentence? What difference is made by the writer presenting his views

73

SCHOLASTIC LITERACY CENTRES

CONT. . .

CONT. . .

through poetry? Ask the children if they understand the *pun* in the title. What does it suggest about the whole idea of being 'civilised' and living in a 'civilisation'? And what might the 'lies' be that are told about civilisation? What Zephaniah is confronting here is the myth that white-populated countries of the northern hemisphere are 'civilised', while Africa is 'uncivilised'. Whereas the truth, we now believe, is that civilisation began in Africa and the Middle East and spread around the world from there.

Read 'How's Dat' (pages 28–9). Racism in all its ugly forms has inspired Zephaniah to write some fierce poems for adult readers. In this collection, he

has a much lighter, naughtier touch when he deals with the subject. The title of this poem is clever: there are various ways to read and understand the phrase, and the Jamaican *dat* instead of the English *that* gives it extra edge (to use a cricketing term). How do the children understand the phrase? It's an appeal; it's a request for clarification; it's a demand for approval, it's a cocky boast. This poem is a response to a question we don't hear, asked by a person we don't know. Can the children explain why such a person would assume a West Indian plays cricket? The thinking goes: West Indians love cricket and are good at it; you are a West Indian; therefore you must play cricket. The word lurking behind this poem is *stereotype*, and it is the essence of racism. How does Zephaniah react to this racial stereotyping? Is this an angry poem? No; what he does is more subtle and understated; he makes fun of the idea, and he begins by making fun of himself. What is he doing in the first part of the poem? He seems to be *apologising* for

being no good at cricket, for being scared. (The word *lick* is lovely, isn't it?) In the second part, what does 'Teacher' say that shows stereotyping in action? And what does Zephaniah say that his people need, more than cricket? He uses *Trigonometry* as a shorthand for what? (Knowledge.)

A poem that really is 'straight-talking' is 'Beyond De Bell' (pages 56–7). Even before they read it, what do the children notice? Those repeated *yu*s scattered across the page like bullet holes. Those heavy *yu*s are like having the author's finger poked at your face. Is this the good-natured, witty voice we hear elsewhere in the book? This is Zephaniah giving a bully a good talking-to in a raw, richly accented voice. Ask the children what else in the poem gives it that punch, that directness. (Short lines, very little metaphor, no 'word-pictures', no regular pattern, no rhyme, no attempt or pretence to speak 'proper' English. When there's a pause, a break, it's not because it's the end of a stanza; it's as if the poet is only pausing for breath.) In the last eight lines, is Zephaniah *really* interested in the answer to

his questions? Is he concerned with the *why* of bullying? When he repeats *What mek yu tink like dat?* does he expect an answer, or is he suggesting that bullies don't think at all?

Drawing on the rhythm of rap poetry, Zephaniah uses list forms in a number of poems. Ask the children to read 'Vegan Delight' (pages 30–1), 'Body Talk' (pages 14–15), 'Greet tings' (pages 12–13) and 'Wordology' (page 43). The list structure here involves bringing everyday items into a poetic form. Point out how 'Body Talk' and 'Vegan Delight' are structured by having a repeating pattern of syllables per line. In each poem ask the children to look at what is listed and how the poem develops the list. 'Wordology' builds up an idea,

playing with two suffixes (*ist* and *cian*); 'Greet tings' lists an array of greetings in different languages and dialects. Whether or not the foods in 'Vegan Delight' are to children's tastes, the words themselves are delicious. Ask the children to read this aloud before you do. How soon do they recognise and use the chant-like rhythm of this list? Can the group hear echoes of other kinds of verse? Doesn't this poem sound rather like a nursery rhyme or a skipping rhyme? Ask the children if they recognise two kinds of rhyme – can they give examples? There are full rhymes, such as *dosa/samosa*, *curd/word*, and there are near-rhymes, such as *nan/uttapam*, *liquoriced/soya dish*. Are the rhyme patterns the same all the way through? How many lines rhyme in the first section? Are the patterns the same in the other two sections?

How does our understanding of the poem change when we read the last two lines? What's the surprise? It is that this list is an answer to a question. As a vegan, Zephaniah is obviously fed up with people saying 'So what

do you eat?' His poem is an answer to this rather stupid question – that there are many things that a vegan can 'delight' in eating.

A number of the poems in this book are short. Ask the children to skim the book, noting down the shorter poems. Can they find the shortest? ('I', page 74.) Read some of the shorter poems together – they make good material for learning and reciting aloud. The length makes them easier to learn and easier to refine if presenting in performance. Focus on 'Multi-Culture' (page 32), 'Who's Who' (pages 48–9), 'Beat It' (page 66), 'I' (page 74) and 'Everyday' (page 87). Examine the playing with words or ideas in each one. For example, look at the play on the word *record* in 'Beat It', and the idea of a birthday each day presented in 'Everyday'. 'Who's Who' and 'I' pack in punchy messages about stereotypes. Finally, ask the group to vote on their favourite shorter poem in the collection.

75

SCHOLASTIC LITERACY CENTRES

ACTIVITY NOTES

Performance readings

Objectives: to read aloud poems, achieving a successful performance; to be aware of the use of different voices in poems; to appreciate the role of rhythm in poems; to be aware of the potential for drama in poems.

Resources: copies of *Talking Turkeys*.

Activity: Because Zephaniah's writing is produced with performance in mind, it would be perverse not to make reading aloud and performing the poems central to your approach to the book. Don't be put off by Zephaniah's use of dialect; the rhythm inherent in the poems isn't a matter of accent.

In several of the poems, such as 'Little Sister' (pages 20–1), 'A Day in the Life of Danny the Cat' (pages 36–9), and 'Rap Connected' (pages 50–1), the typography suggests the way in which a whole-class reading might be divided between individual and choral voices. Poems such as 'A Killer Lies' (pages 52–3) and 'For Sale' (pages 62–3) also offer opportunities for using more than one voice, although without obvious typographical cues. 'Food for Thought' (page 33) is almost a script for a little satirical playlet; try using a couple of picture frames to represent TV screens, and confer with the children as to how different voices in the poem might be represented.

Title search

Objectives: to identify poems written in different forms; to understand the meanings of titles.

Resources: photocopiable page 82, copies of *Talking Turkeys*, writing materials.

Activity: The photocopiable sheet is a simple quiz. Ask the children to scan the collection and write appropriate titles in the spaces on the sheet.

The answers are: 1. 'Greet tings' (pages 12–13) or 'Body Talk' (pages 14–15) or 'Vegan Delight' (pages 30–1) or 'Wordology' (page 43); 2. 'Everyday' (page 87); 3. 'Once Upon a Time' (page 93); 4. 'Royal Tea' (pages 26–7) or 'Drivosaurus Rex' (pages 40–1) or 'Civil Lies' (pages 58–9) or 'Pets Control' (page 67) or 'Eye See' (pages 84–5); 5. 'Beyond de Bell' (pages 56–7); 6. 'Civil Lies' (pages 58–9); 7. 'Royal Tea' (pages 26–7) or 'A Beetle called Derek' (pages 64–5); 8. 'De Generation Rap' (pages 44–5) or 'Rap Connected' (pages 50–1) or 'Heroes' (pages 54–5); 9. 'Food for Thought' (page 33); 10. 'I' (page 74); 11. 'Jude' (page 81); 12. 'Open Market' (page 32). (Children might insist on alternative answers, which is fine if they can argue their case!)

An edible poem

Objectives: to read a poem carefully, paying particular attention to its rhythmic structure; to use that structure as a basis for new writing.

Resources: photocopiable page 83, copies of *Talking Turkeys*, writing materials.

Activity: Ask the children to read or re-read Zephaniah's 'Vegan Delight' (pages 30–1), listening carefully to its chanting rhythm. On the photocopiable sheet there is the beginning of a different list of foods; ask the children to add more – each item in no more than three words. They can do this working independently or in pairs. Encourage them to continue the list until they have used all the space provided. They should then try to use their list to continue the list poem, maintaining the rhythm that is similar to 'Vegan Delight', and keeping the rhyme. Point out that to do this, they may need to add or omit words, as in the example, where *spicy* has been added to *chicken tikka*, and *oven chips* has been shortened to *chips*.

Some children may realise that that the ordering of the list depends on the number of stressed syllables in each line (alternately three and two); that is less important than their ability to hear and follow the rhythm – they may find that chanting their words or tapping on the table is helpful.

Extension: Challenge the children to write a list poem in the same way, but using imaginary horrible foods such as *slugs on toast, Brussels sprouts milk shake, French flies*.

Write the school's lunch menu for the week as a list poem; or compile a pretend one, with items such as *Tuesday is alligator stew day*.

A poetic licence

Objectives: to appreciate the linguistic and typographical devices in a poem; to create a piece of work in response to a poem.

Resources: copies of *Talking Turkeys*, paper, writing and colouring materials.

Activity: Explain the concept of 'poetic licence' – that is, that poets somehow have permission to write things that are not strictly true and use language in ways that are 'incorrect'. Read or re-read 'According to My Mood' (pages 24–5) and discuss the way that Zephaniah uses it as a justification for linguistic and typographical wordplay (for example, the spelling of *write* instead of *right* in *I do my spelling write*, and *rong* for *wrong* in *I can't go rong*; the repetition of *I repeat when I like*; the placing of the extra commas and brackets in lines 8 and 9).

What do the children think Zephaniah is saying about poetic licence in the end? How does the last line tell us that he is sending up the idea? Who might say: 'Don't question me?' (Someone who knows he's wrong.)

Ask the children to draw up their own 'poetic licence' in the form of an 'official document' which lists the liberties the licence holder can take with language and truth. They could take ideas from 'According to My Mood' and/or invent their own. They might adapt some of Zephaniah's ideas, claim the right to write upside down, miss letters out of words, and so on. Point out that poetic licence also permits exaggeration and nonsense, such as calling a spade a violin or comparing the sky to buttered toast.

Suggest that they use impressive lettering for the heading, add a drawing or photo of themselves and include 'official' phraseology, such as *This is to certify that...* [name]; *and is hereby entitled to...* They can then decorate their completed permits, as appropriate. Alternatively, they could produce their poetic licences at the computer.

Wild words and wheelbarrows

Objective: to examine some of the textual devices used by Benjamin Zephaniah and apply them to a poem by Adrian Mitchell.

Resources: photocopiable page 84, copies of *Talking Turkeys* and *The Thirteen Secrets of Poetry*, writing and colouring materials.

Activity: Ask the children to read Benjamin Zephaniah's 'De Generation Rap' (pages 44–5) and consider the way the physical appearance of words can seem to echo their meanings, for example the small italic script of *easy*, the fat, plain bold font used for *tuff*. Are there words that could have been made more interesting? How else might *Big up* have been printed? How might *wild* have been a bit wilder?

The photocopiable sheet provides a cloze of part of Adrian Mitchell's 'The Wildest Wheelbarrow' (Secret One). The children should supply the missing words, but give them the 'Zephaniah' treatment. For example, *Wildest* might be in a crazy assortment of letter styles and colours; *wonky* might have its letters 'falling about' at different angles. If the children can think of their own words rather than use Mitchell's for the cloze, that would be excellent.

Make a display of the end results. (You may have chosen to assign different lines from the poem to different children and combine the outcomes.)

Extension: Children may have fun applying this activity to other poems, such as Benjamin Zephaniah's 'Movie Madness' (pages 78–9) or, from the Adrian Mitchell anthology, 'Listening' (Secret Seven) or 'The Wind Has Such a Rainy Sound' (Secret Twelve).

Heroes

Objective: to understand the ideas in a poem and use them as a basis for new writing.

Resources: copies of *Talking Turkeys*, writing materials.

Activity: The first part of this activity could be conducted with the whole class; the writing part could be undertaken by pairs or groups of children. Read 'Heroes' (pages 54–5). What is a hero? Traditionally, heroes are people who succeed against enormous odds or overcome supernatural enemies, like the characters in ancient mythology. But what does the word mean to children now? What words can the children offer to describe what we feel towards someone who is a hero: *admiration, respect, envy, worship*? Are heroes people we want to be like? What kinds of people does Benjamin Zephaniah describe as heroic? Are some of them surprising? Can the children think of examples for some of these types?

Ask the children to think of and collect names of heroes. Encourage them to go beyond the fields of sport and music into, for example, myth and legend, both ancient and modern (Robin Hood, Batman); history and politics (Florence Nightingale, Nelson Mandela, Martin Luther King, Ghandi). Fictional heroes, from comics, TV and cartoons, as well as books, can be included, too. Ask the children to think about and note down the different qualities and abilities of their heroes. Challenge them to combine them in a list or rap poem. The first four lines could be: [Name of famous footballer]*'s a hero / He's great on the pitch and knows how to score / Robin Hood's a hero / He took from the rich and gave to the poor.*

Connected

Objective: to use the text and page layout of a poem to stimulate new writing.

Resources: photocopiable page 85, copies of *Talking Turkeys*, writing materials.

Activity: Read 'Rap Connected' (pages 50–1). The point that Zephaniah is making in this poem is, of course, that peoples seemingly divided by class, or culture or race share a common humanity which 'connects' them. The way the poem is presented on the page is as significant as the text itself. The poem's thesis is reinforced by the way that the speech bubbles are connected, and by the fact that the 'talking heads' on the page are symbolic of very different kinds of people. (There's a nice joke implied by having a cartoon granny figure speaking the words *We got riddim in us mate*.)

The photocopiable sheet features four different 'speakers'. Ask the children to write lines in the bubbles which might reflect the personality of each speaker or – as a more demanding activity – lines which are comically incongruous. The second and third bubbles require more inventiveness than the first and fourth. Children should steal ideas from the original text without merely repeating them.

The last person on earth

Objective: to read a sequence of related poems and identify their themes and the issues they raise.

Resources: photocopiable page 86, copies of *Talking Turkeys*, writing materials.

Activity: Ask the children to read, silently, the six 'Poems from the Last Person on Earth' (pages 62–71). Two of the shorter poems may need some explanation. 'Beat It' (page 66) contains a familiar pun on 'breaking records', but what has it to do with ecology? The record was a *world record* – and one possible meaning of the phrase is 'a history of the world or a list of all that was in it'. In other words, the record is a *symbol* for the world. This has been broken – destroyed – and that's something to boast about (*I am famous for it*) at first. But without *music* – life, pleasure – things can get a bit boring. 'Think Me' (pages 70–1) relates to the title of this sequence of poems. We live in other people's memories; what happens when there's no one left to do any remembering? When Zephaniah says he wants to be *In someone's mind* he's hoping that *someone* will survive.

The photocopiable sheet is a simple grid on which the children should try to record, using 'bullets' or ticks or crosses in the appropriate boxes, the issues which appear in this sequence of poems. The 'answers' are not all clear-cut; if children mark surprising spaces on the grid, that's fine if they are able to argue the case.

Extension: Children could expand this grid onto a larger sheet by identifying and adding themes from other Zephaniah poems onto the vertical axis, and titles onto the horizontal.

Save the turkey

Objectives: to explore the persuasiveness of a poem; to compare the poem with a prose piece on the same theme; to use both to produce a campaign poster.

Resources: photocopiable page 87, copies of *Talking Turkeys,* A3 (or larger) paper, writing and colouring materials.

Activity: Ask the children to read Benjamin Zephaniah's poem 'Talking Turkeys!!' (pages 88–9) and then the text on the photocopiable sheet. Discuss with the children what both are trying to do, and which, in their opinions, is more likely to be successful (at persuading people not to eat turkeys). The poem is comical – does that mean that it must be less persuasive? What is the significance of the words *'for life'* in the poem? Which of the two pieces of writing are we likely to remember best?

Next, ask the children, working in pairs, to:

■ underline in *green* the statements in the prose text which match or resemble parts of Zephaniah's poem

SCHOLASTIC LITERACY CENTRES

■ underline in *red* statements in the prose text which the children find especially persuasive.
(Resemblances might include: *talking/complicated vocabulary; Mum/females are very protective mothers; caged up/kept in huge sheds; genetically made up/unnaturally huge*.)

Finally, ask the children to use both texts, or parts of both, to create a campaign poster aimed at persuading people not to eat turkey. How might the poem and the factual material be juxtaposed? What slogans and additional text might the children want to include? How would the poster be illustrated and designed?

Extension: Children could use the information on the photocopiable sheet to write extra lines or verses for 'Talking Turkeys!!'.

Christmas with Benji

Objectives: to re-read the collection, gathering ideas and information which help the reader to understand more about the poet; to present poetry in a different form.

Resources: photocopiable page 88, copies of *Talking Turkeys*, writing materials.

Activity: Ask the children to complete the photocopiable sheet, which shows Benjamin Zephaniah's 'Christmas planner', including his 'wish list' of presents. Some parts of the schedule may be completed by gleaning information from the poems in the book, while others may require the children to use their imagination based on what they have learned about the poet and his likes, dislikes and beliefs. Who will his dinner guests be? Why won't the hedgehog be among them? Ask the children to work some of Danny the Cat's routines into the day.

How many secrets of Benjamin Zephaniah?

Objective: to see how many of the poems in *Talking Turkeys* match the 'secrets' criteria in *The Thirteen Secrets of Poetry*.

Resources: copies of *Talking Turkeys* and *The Thirteen Secrets of Poetry*, paper, writing materials.

Activity: Ask the children, working individually, to read through the 'secrets' boxes on the left-hand pages of *The Thirteen Secrets of Poetry*. Then, taking the 'secrets' one at a time, they should re-scan *Talking Turkeys* and see if there are poems which match these criteria. They should record their matches, using two columns to arrange the information, for example:

Mitchell	Zephaniah
Secret One: Use your feet To find the beat.	*'Vegan Delight'*

Children will no doubt find that some of Mitchell's 'secrets' match more than one of Zephaniah's poems, while others don't match any. There are few absolutely right or wrong matches, but the children should be able to express their reasons for making their decisions.

Pictures for poems

Objective: to choose a poem and illustrate it in a way that shows an awareness of its meaning.

Resources: copies of *Talking Turkeys*, paper, writing and art materials.

Activity: What can the children say about the way the collection is illustrated? Are there any original, hand-drawn images? Where have many of these images been clipped from? (Old books and magazines.) Some are mixed up into collages, such as on pages 68–9 and on page 82. Do the children find them interesting? Do they always reflect the content of the poems?

If the children feel that Zephaniah's colourful poems deserve colourful illustration, now's their chance. Ask the children to choose a short poem (or part of a longer poem) to illustrate. They might use conventional art materials, or make collages from magazine photographs, or (if they have the facilities and know how to use them) they could use drawing/clip art/desktop publishing programmes on a computer. Whatever methods are used, encourage the children to read the poem carefully a number of times before they begin, and to let the words suggest the images they use.

Talking pictures

Objective: to comment on illustrations to poems and how they relate to the text.

Resources: photocopiable page 89, copies of *Talking Turkeys*, writing materials.

Activity: The photocopiable sheet reproduces images from the book. The children should identify the poems which they illustrate and in each writing space provided say what the image conjures up for them, how it links to the poem, and whether they think it is a good illustration. The illustrations have been taken from 'Civil Lies' (pages 58–9), 'Heroes' (pages 54–5), 'Once Upon A Time' (page 93) and 'According to My Mood' (pages 24–5).

Part tings

Objective: to compile a list poem which could end *Talking Turkeys*.

Resources: photocopiable page 90, copies of *Talking Turkeys*, foreign language dictionaries or phrase books, writing materials.

Activity: Working in groups or pairs, the children should collect as many words for *goodbye* in as many languages as they can find. (If your class makes use of the local public library, this part of the activity might be done there.)

Tell the children that they can expand their lists by using English colloquial words and phrases such as *ta-ra; cheerio; see ya; mind how you go;* and so on. All these words and phrases should be collected on the grid on the photocopiable sheet.

When the children have completed their grids, they should cut along the dotted lines, and experiment with ordering the words or phrases until they find a pleasing pattern of rhythm and sound emerging. Explain that in doing so, they will be creating a list poem in the manner of 'Greet tings' (page 13).

Once they are satisfied with their ordering, their list poems can either be copied out or gummed onto a fresh sheet of paper – and maybe illustrated, too.

Extension: Try combining – perhaps with some editing – the children's poems into one large class poster.

Name _____ Date _____

Title search

Benjamin Zephaniah writes poems in lots of different forms. Look through *Talking Turkeys* and find a poem which fits each of these descriptions. Write the titles here.

1. A list poem _____

2. A shape poem _____

3. A poem with a title that sounds like the beginning of a fairy story _____

4. A poem with a title that's a pun _____

5. A dramatic monologue _____

6. A poem that's a letter _____

7. A narrative poem _____

8. A rap poem _____

9. A poem that's an advert _____

10. A thin poem _____

11. A limerick _____

12. A poem that's a shop receipt _____

Name _____   Date _____

An edible poem

Read 'Vegan Delight'. Can you hear the rhythm in it? On the left side of this
sheet, a list of foods has been started. Add things you like to eat. Then try to
continue the poem on the right, using the foods on your list. Keep the rhythm!

oven chips
pepperoni pizza
garlic bread
carrots
tomato sauce
cheese
mushy peas
chicken tikka

Spicy chicken tikka
Mushy peas
Pepperoni pizza
Chips and cheese

_____

_____

_____

_____

_____

_____

_____

_____

_____

_____

_____

_____

_____

_____

_____

_____

_____

Name

Date

Wild words and wheelbarrows

Read Benjamin Zephaniah's 'De Generation Rap' and Adrian Mitchell's 'The Wildest Wheelbarrow'. Design wild-looking words to fill the gaps in this part of Adrian Mitchell's poem.

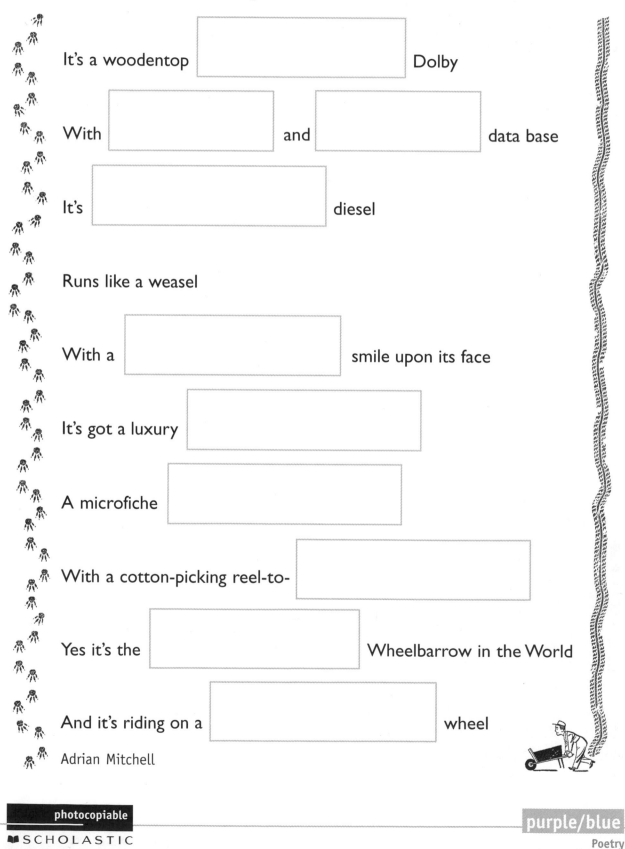

It's a woodentop [ ] Dolby

With [ ] and [ ] data base

It's [ ] diesel

Runs like a weasel

With a [ ] smile upon its face

It's got a luxury [ ]

A microfiche [ ]

With a cotton-picking reel-to- [ ]

Yes it's the [ ] Wheelbarrow in the World

And it's riding on a [ ] wheel

Adrian Mitchell

SCHOLASTIC LITERACY CENTRES

Name _____   Date _____

Connected

We were born to _____

_____

We were born to _____

_____

We were born to _____

_____

_____

We are _____

_____

_____

_____

_____

We are connected.

SCHOLASTIC LITERACY CENTRES

photocopiable

SCHOLASTIC

Name _____   Date _____

The last person on earth

Read the poems in the 'Poems from the Last Person on Earth' section of
Talking Turkeys (pages 62 to 71). Using the grid, mark which of the
environmental issues feature in the poems.

Poems

Issues	'For Sale'	'A Beetle called Derek'	'Beat It'	'Pets Control'	'Memories'	'Think Me'
Extinction						
The ozone layer						
Pollution						
Cutting down forests						
Diet						
Cruelty to animals						
Climate change						

SCHOLASTIC LITERACY CENTRES

Name   Date

Save the turkey

To most people turkeys are a joke – the very word is a term of abuse. But there's a lot more to turkeys than most of us realise. Wild turkeys are still found in the Americas, where they live in open forest. They have a complicated vocabulary of calls which they use to let other birds know about dangers, and to communicate contentment when they are together in safe groups. Nesting in trees, females are very protective mothers, and never abandon either eggs or chicks if predators approach.

Turkeys aren't just for Christmas anymore – about 30 million are killed and eaten throughout the year. The turkeys are kept in huge sheds – up to 25000 in one dark windowless building. Wild turkeys can run at speeds of up to 20mph, and can fly at speeds of 50 to 55mph. Farmed turkeys become so unnaturally huge that they have difficulty walking.

Many intensively reared turkeys die in the sheds because of the poor conditions in which they're kept – intensive rearing is a very wasteful process. The birds who survive are packed into crates and sent off to the slaughterhouse. They are hung upside down from a conveyer belt and stunned by having their heads dipped into an electrically charged water bath but sometimes they pull up their heads and miss the water completely. Then an automatic knife slits their throats whether they are stunned or not. Most are killed but some are only injured. The birds are then plunged into a tank of scalding water – this is to make it easier to pluck off their feathers. Turkeys do feel pain, of course.

Do you really want to eat turkey this Christmas?

From a letter to a newspaper, December 2001

SCHOLASTIC LITERACY CENTRES

Name

Date

Christmas with Benji

This is Benjamin Zephaniah's Christmas Day diary. Flip through *Talking Turkeys* and find ways to fill it in for him. What does he want from Santa? What does he have for breakfast? When does he see his little sister, and what does he give her? Where is his Christmas tree? Who comes for Christmas dinner, and what do they eat? What does Danny the Cat do all day?

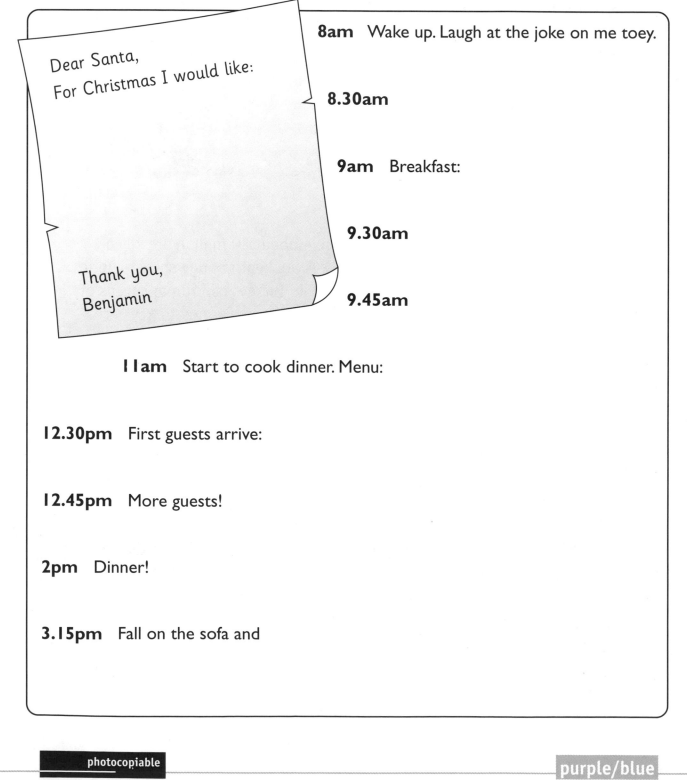

8am Wake up. Laugh at the joke on me toey.

8.30am

9am Breakfast:

9.30am

9.45am

Dear Santa,
For Christmas I would like:

Thank you,
Benjamin

11am Start to cook dinner. Menu:

12.30pm First guests arrive:

12.45pm More guests!

2pm Dinner!

3.15pm Fall on the sofa and

Name _____ Date _____

Talking pictures

These pictures illustrate four poems from *Talking Turkeys*. First look through the book and find the title of each poem. Then write beside each one what you think of the illustration. Does it fit the poem? Why do you think it was chosen?

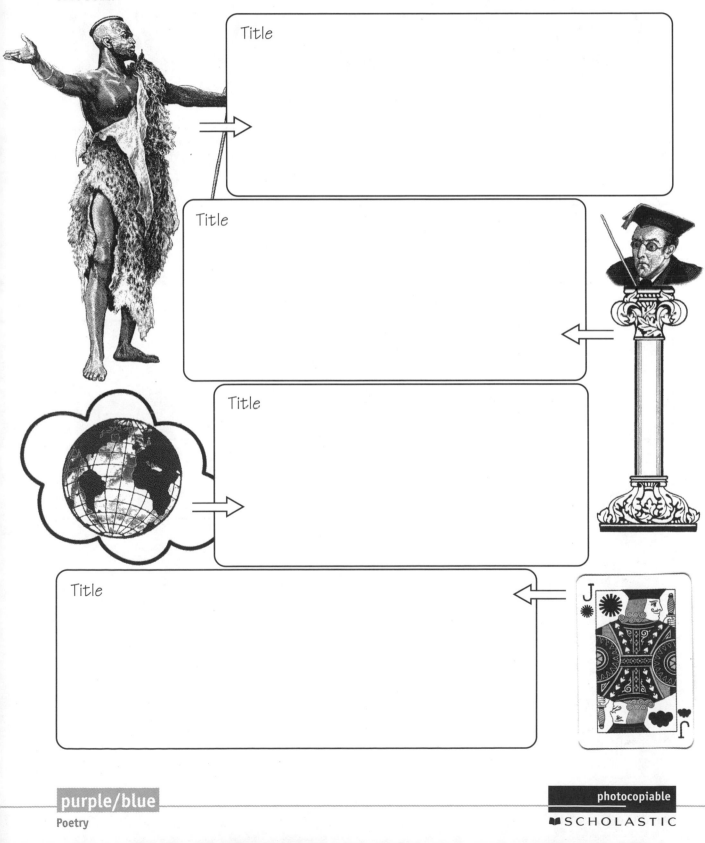

Title

Title

Title

Title

Name   Date

Part tings

Write in this grid as many foreign words for **goodbye** as you can find. Then add as many **English** words or phrases for **goodbye** as you can think of. Cut along the dotted lines and arrange your goodbyes in an order that sounds as good as Benjamin Zephaniah's 'Greet tings'.

Interviewing Benjamin Zephaniah

Background

Benjamin Zephaniah is generous with his time when being asked about his work; he has given many interviews, works with children a great deal, and comes across as both modest and honest. Here, he talks about being an 'oral' (that is, performance) poet and how that makes his poetry different from 'printed' poetry.

There's a significant connection in this text between what Zephaniah says about his work within the oral tradition and what Berlie Doherty states in her foreword to *The Forsaken Merman: The Wayland Book of Story Poems* and the poems she chooses for her anthology. The oral tradition, Zephaniah insists, is very much alive, not a thing of the past, in this age of the Internet.

But is he right to insist on such a great divide between 'real life', 'uplifting' poetry and 'printed' poetry? Can poetry not be both?

■ Ensure that the children understand what the 'oral tradition' is (see section A of photocopiable page 93). They will already be familiar with it, with things that mysteriously become known before they are written down. Can they give examples, for example traditional tales and fairy stories, nursery, skipping and counting rhymes, jokes, gossip, proverbs, superstitions?

Suggest that families have their own oral traditions, and see if the children can explain what that means – that families have unwritten stories (constantly embroidered, probably) about relatives, holidays, all sorts of events.

■ Zephaniah says that the oral tradition still thrives in certain situations. Encourage the children to give examples of what these might be, such as when there is censorship, when people have no radio or TV or when they cannot read.

■ In section C, what might Zephaniah mean by the word *accessible*? Can the children define it? *Is* his poetry accessible? Can they suggest kinds of people who might *not* find it so?

■ Zephaniah says (section E) that 'Who's Who' (page 48 in *Talking Turkeys*) has a lot to say about the kind of person he used to be. Ask the children to explore the comment. Zephaniah is admitting to having preconceptions about groups of people and that it was only by joining one of those groups that he realised his assumptions were wrong. That he uses police and nurses as examples is revealing – these people wear uniforms, and might seem (to unthinking people) to have no individuality.

■ Provide the children with *Talking Turkeys* and photocopiable page 93 in order for them to complete photocopiable page 94. Use photocopiable page 94 to explore the idea of what is 'simple' in poetry. The poem 'Who's Who' is about stereotyping, and the underlying layers of it are more complicated than you would first assume. Before the children attempt to answer the questions on the photocopiable sheet, make sure that they understand the meaning of the word *stereotype*. Can they offer a definition? Talk about how Zephaniah is reacting against people being 'pigeonholed', against certain groups of people being perceived as all the same. (You could also revisit 'How's Dat' on pages 28–9 to explore further this idea.) Can the children think of other people who could be sterotyped: football supporters or farmers, for example?

■ Returning to photocopiable page 93, discuss the tricky words in section D and encourage the children

CONT. . .

92

CONT. . .

to decide on meanings for them: *academic, Oxford, obsessed, poetic form, dissect, intellectualisation*. Stay with that last word: doesn't it describe what *all* readers (including ourselves) do? Talk about poems, think about what they mean, read things into them? Is Benjamin Zephaniah being a bit bossy when he says we shouldn't do that? And is he right to make fun of someone who thinks something is beautiful but doesn't understand it? Don't we often feel that way about a painting or music, for example?

■ Ask the children what they notice about the way Zephaniah uses language in these interviews compared with the way he writes in *Talking Turkeys*. It's obvious that he has at least two voices: the direct, accented, simple language of the poems; and this sophisticated version of standard English. Can the children see the great advantage it gives *anyone* to be able to vary their 'voice' according to their audience? They may wish to pursue this when they are working on photocopiable page 95, which asks them to imagine being a journalist preparing to interview Benjamin Zephaniah. Some research will be necessary for the potted biography (the Internet has a good deal of information).

■ Photocopiable page 96 is more challenging: it asks children to *be* Benjamin Zephaniah responding to interview questions. Point out to the children that the poems themselves provide as many answers as the interview extracts on photocopiable page 93 do.

assessment

ASSESSMENT NOTES

Design a Zephaniah flyer

Assessment focus: to convey concisely the appeal of the poet's work and personality in the form of a publicity handout.
Resources: photocopiable page 97, paper, writing and art materials.
Activity: Ask the children to imagine that they work for a publicity company and have been asked to design a flyer advertising a performance by Benjamin Zephaniah at the school. Explain that a flyer is a miniature poster which can be handed out in the street, posted through letterboxes, pinned on noticeboards, and so on. The photocopiable sheet is a 'design brief' which children should work through and then go on to produce their flyers. Unless the children want to include a quotation in their design, reference to the book should not be necessary.

Question and quotation

Assessment focus: to demonstrate understanding of Benjamin Zephaniah's beliefs; to cite appropriate passages of text to support answers.
Resources: photocopiable page 98, copies of *Talking Turkeys,* writing materials.
Activity: The questions on the photocopiable sheet are simple yes/no options; ask the children to draw a circle around or underline the correct answer. They should be able to support their choices with short quotations from the poems and supply a page number reference. Since some answers could be supported by a number of quotes, encourage the children to select the one they think the best, rather than the first one they find.

Interviewing Benjamin Zephaniah

A The oral tradition is timeless, it is simply the tradition of passing on information orally and much of this information is handed down in the form of poems, songs and stories. People in the western world tend to see the oral tradition as something from the past and not relevant in the age of the Internet, but elsewhere the tradition carries on regardless. The oral tradition thrives when there are restrictions on people's abilities to speak or when they have no access to the media.

from www.oneworld.org/zephaniah/oral_poetry.html

B I was never a great reader and learnt to read and write late, so I always like to hear poetry, as opposed to reading it.

from www.youngwriter.org

93

SCHOLASTIC LITERACY CENTRES

C I would say that the poet's role was to question things in an accessible way and to raise people's spirits. I want to use accessible, everyday speech in my poetry and it's great when people hear my poetry and say, "Oh, it's so simple! I wish I could've written that!" That's the only ability I have really... to wrap things up in a way that it means something to people and articulate it in a positive way.

Interview: Ian Burns for *The Argotist* online magazine at www.geocities.com/SoHo/Den/3776/arg9.html

D I heard recently about one academic at Oxford who's absolutely obsessed with poetic form and he read a poem on television and said it was a beautiful poem with beautiful form and the words ran beautifully... but he didn't even know what it was on about! He didn't understand it! That's what's so different about the written form as opposed to the oral tradition. With the written form, people read it, dissect it, try to read other things into it. I'm against that intellectualisation of poetry. I've seen people do it with my poetry and I'm like, "whaat?" I live in the real world. To me, it's more important that a poem has form when you say it, using the rhythm of everyday life. Context to me is always important. The big question must always be, "What does it have to do with our real lives?"

Interview: Ian Burns for *The Argotist* online magazine at www.geocities.com/SoHo/Den/3776/arg9.html

E My most favourite piece is a small poem called 'Who's Who', and although it's short I find it really says a lot about the kind of person I used to be.

from www.youngwriter.org

(See also www.benjaminzephaniah.com)

Name _____   Date _____

Who's Who

In 'Interviewing Benjamin Zephaniah', he mentions a poem called 'Who's Who'. It's on page 48 of *Talking Turkeys*. Read it, then try to complete the question trail below.

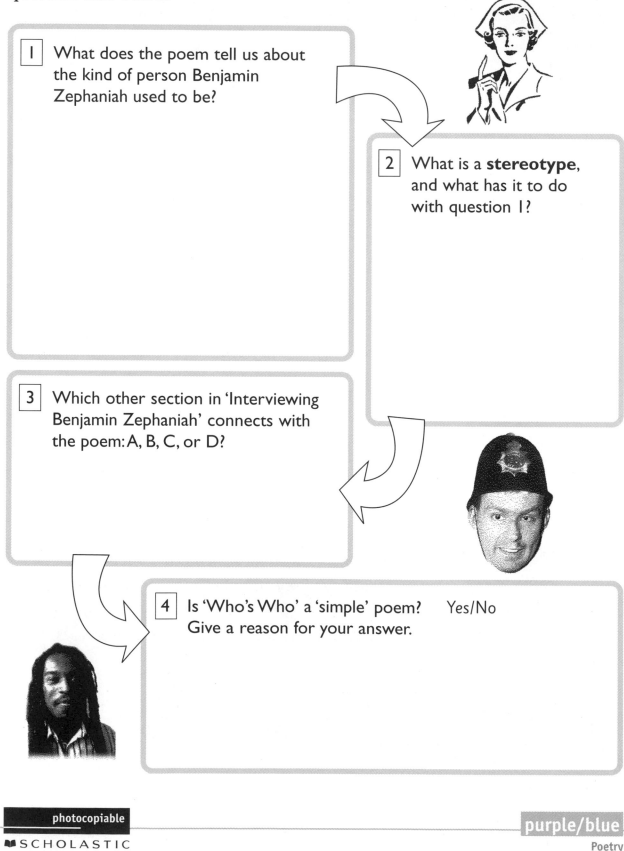

| 1 | What does the poem tell us about the kind of person Benjamin Zephaniah used to be? |

| 2 | What is a **stereotype**, and what has it to do with question 1? |

| 3 | Which other section in 'Interviewing Benjamin Zephaniah' connects with the poem: A, B, C, or D? |

| 4 | Is 'Who's Who' a 'simple' poem?   Yes/No   Give a reason for your answer. |

Name   Date

A job for you

Memo

From: the editor

To: _____

I want you to interview the poet Benjamin Zephaniah tomorrow. Before you leave today, I need you to send me a short potted biography of the guy (include a couple of his best-known titles please) plus 6 questions you plan to ask him.

Thanks,
E.

Biographical sketch:

Question 1: _____

_____

Question 2: _____

_____

Question 3: _____

_____

Question 4: _____

_____

Question 5: _____

_____

Question 6: _____

_____

Name _____ Date _____

Being Benjamin Zephaniah

For this activity you have to imagine that you are Benjamin Zephaniah and that you are being interviewed for a magazine. Here are some of the questions the interviewer asks you. How do you answer?

1. *Is music important to you? Does it help you to write poetry?*

_____

_____

_____

2. *You're famous for your live poetry performances. Do you think your poems work just as well printed in a book? Can they have the same energy on the page as on the stage?*

_____

_____

_____

3. *In* Talking Turkeys *you poke fun at racism. Why is that? Racism isn't really funny, is it?*

_____

_____

_____

4. *Many of your poems are about issues: the environment, peace, not eating animals, and so on. Do you think poets can change the world?*

_____

_____

_____

5. *What would you say to someone who said your poems were too simple?*

_____

_____

_____

Name

Date

Design a Zephaniah flyer

○ Class Act Design Ltd ○

Design brief

Project:	A flyer to announce performance by poet Benjamin Zephaniah.
Size:	Small enough to be a street handout. Big enough for key words to be legible from 2m.
Colour:	Bright. Green? Are there special Rastafarian colours? Keep simple, though.
Typography:	Plain and simple, easily read? Or a bit wild to suggest Zephaniah's energy and style? Mix of both?
Text:	Place and date, of course. BZ's name biggest text. Avoid 'poetry reading'. 'Performance by' maybe. Any ideas? How to describe BZ? 'Rap poet'? 'Dub poet'? Find me some words to excite people's interest. Use phrase 'Talk Turkey' maybe?
Visuals:	Not much space. Photo/cartoon of BZ? Those dreadlocks are almost a trademark – can we design them in?

I need this by the end of the week, please! Cheers, Jo

Name   Date

Question and quotation

Choose **Yes** or **No** as your answer to each of these questions. Support each choice with a short quotation from one of the poems in *Talking Turkeys*, and write down the number of the page where you found it.

---

1. Do you think Benjamin Zephaniah would enjoy a cheeseburger?

Quote: Yes   No

                                                   Page

---

2. Has Benjamin Zephaniah ever played cricket?

Quote: Yes   No

                                                   Page

---

3. Would Benjamin Zephaniah buy his girlfriend a fur coat?

Quote: Yes   No

                                                   Page

---

4. Do you think Benjamin Zephaniah would go fox-hunting?

Quote: Yes   No

                                                   Page

---

5. Does Benjamin Zephaniah like zoos?

Quote: Yes   No

                                                   Page

---

6. Would Benjamin Zephaniah prefer you to plant a tree for him rather than buy him a Christmas present?

Quote: Yes   No

                                                   Page

SCHOLASTIC LITERACY CENTRES

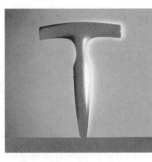

HE FORSAKEN MERMAN: THE WAYLAND BOOK OF STORY POEMS
SELECTED BY BERLIE DOHERTY

About the book

This collection is a hearty meal tucked into a small lunchbox. There are 58 poems and extracts in this book, together comprising a terrific variety of forms and flavours. And this is as it should be, because 'story poetry' – or narrative verse, to give the genre its more scholarly title – is a catch-all category; the *only* identifying characteristic of a narrative verse is that it tells a story. So, happily, Berlie Doherty has plundered widely; she has included traditional (sung) ballads (for example, 'The Dying Cowboy'), poetic (written) ballads (for example, 'Overheard in County Sligo'), dramatic monologues, dialect verse, classic verse, parodies and adaptations, choral poems and modern free-verse narratives. There's comedy, mystery, tragedy, fable and legend. There's complaining, celebrating, clowning and grieving. There ought to be something here for all tastes.

There's a continuity in this selection, too. In her foreword, Berlie Doherty alludes to the oral tradition from which narrative poetry evolved. The form which retains this tradition most obviously is the ballad, and the ballad form, the ballad stanza, runs through this anthology – sometimes in disguise. What's significant about it is that it evolved to be easily memorable by people who didn't read. So it is a simple form: four rhythmic lines, two of them rhyming. This simplicity makes it adaptable, too. A ballad can be added to, improvised and updated so long as you maintain that four-line structure.

Traditional ballads are usually anonymous, for the obvious reason that they weren't originally written at all. Examples in this collection are 'Robin Hood and Alan a Dale' and 'Sir Patrick Spens'. But the elasticity of the form encouraged poets to take it up. Longfellow's 'The Wreck of the Hesperus' and Keats' 'La Belle Dame Sans Merci' stick close to the conventional form; Lewis Carroll's 'Jabberwocky' makes nonsense of it; Walter de la Mare's 'The Listeners' disguises it by running the stanzas together; in 'Overheard in County Sligo' Gillian Clarke updates and subdues it.

This book is also a collection of short stories in verse, packed with incidents and characters, and told in a multiplicity of voices.

About the compiler

Berlie Doherty is a highly versatile writer – a novelist, poet and screenwriter who is adept in several genres and whose readership spans a wide age range. There's a strong element of legend and fantasy running through her work, but she also engages with some tough social issues. She works with children a good deal, and has initiated an interactive website novel. Two of her novels, *Granny was a Buffer Girl* and *Dear Nobody,* won Carnegie Medals.

GUIDED READING NOTES

Begin by reading Berlie Doherty's foreword. Ask the children how far back in time Doherty is taking us in the first paragraph, when she talks about minstrels and stories sung or recited at village gatherings. (Several hundred years, before most people could read, and before there were newspapers and books.) Do the children know the phrase *oral tradition*, used to describe stories kept alive by being learned by heart and passed on? Doherty talks of the *music of poetry*; in what other ways might rhythm and rhyme help maintain the oral tradition? Can the children pick out the different things that Doherty says about the subjects of story poems?

Read 'The Lion and Albert' (pages 14–17) because it's good to begin with some fun. Read the poem, then explain that this is a famous *comic monologue* from the days of music halls, which means that comedians learned and recited it. Can the children identify features of its regular form which might make it easy to memorise?

We shouldn't need to labour the jokes here, but you might introduce the terms *irony* and *ironic understatement*. Irony, in this case, is the comic mismatch between what is done and how it is described, as in *nothing to laugh at at all* (stanza 3); *brave*, meaning 'stupid' (stanza 7). Ironic understatement describes the whole poem, really, but in particular the madly inappropriate, underwhelmed way in which the adults react to Albert being eaten. Can the children pick out individual phrases which demonstrate this? (For example, *'Well, I am vexed!'*; *'What a nasty mishap.'*)

There are other comic poems in the collection: 'The Burglar' (page 36), 'Mr Simpson and His Cat' (pages 82–5), 'Jack and the Beanstalk' (pages 100–4), 'The Mouse Song' (pages 173–5). Ask the group to read one or two and to comment on them briefly in the next session.

Familiarise the children with the conventional ballad stanza. The best way is to sample a number of ballads and note their resemblances. Try reading the first few stanzas from two or three of the following: 'Robin Hood and Alan a Dale' (pages 37–41), 'The Wreck of the Hesperus' (pages 69–72), 'Sir Patrick Spens' (pages 86–8), 'La Belle Dame Sans Merci' (pages 105–6), 'Harry Eddom' (pages 111–12). See if the children can spot three things they have in common. (Four lines; the first and third slightly longer; the pattern of end-rhymes.) Help them to hear and count the rhythm each has by exaggerating the four beats (stressed syllables) in the longer lines and the three in the shorter, for example:

As **Rob** in **Hood** in the **for**est **stood**,
All **un** der the **green**-wood **tree**,
There he was **ware** of a **brave** young **man**,
As **fine** as **fine** might **be**.

Often, as in the stanza above, there are familiar 'tricks' used to give extra strength to stressed syllables by making them more noticeable. Can the children say what these are? (Repetition/alliteration, as in *fine... fine*; internal rhyme, as in *Hood... stood*.)

Can the children make a connection between the regular rhythm of the ballad stanza and the oral tradition discussed earlier? Can they grasp that having this repeating pattern in one's head makes memorising easier?

Read one or two poems which use the ballad stanza in less obvious ways – De La Mare's tantalising and mysterious 'The Listeners' (pages 33–5), for example. Do the children think this looks like a ballad? Ask them to cover all the lines except the first four with a sheet of paper. Now do they recognise the 4, 3, 4, 3 pattern of beats, the rhymes, and the use of alliteration (in line 4) to give the rhythm extra thump? Uncover the next four lines: don't they follow the

same pattern? This poem is a ballad in disguise; all that's missing is the spaces between the stanzas. Read the whole poem, and explore its ghostly, spooky atmosphere.

'Overheard in County Sligo' (page 44) is a quietly spoken tale of disappointment and loneliness set in modern Ireland. The ballad stanza's rhythm and rhymes are there still, but much more subdued; can the children still hear them? Who is the narrator, and what can the children say about her character and her feelings? Can they suggest why a quieter kind of ballad is more appropriate to her voice than a tumpety-tump variety such as 'Robin Hood and Alan a Dale'?

'Jabberwocky' (pages 63–4) is a nonsense poem, but of what kind? Can the children detect an adventure-story ballad – one about a daring knight and a dreadful dragon – seen through the distorting mirror of Carroll's mad vocabulary? They may not make sense of the first stanza, but can they test it against the ballad stanza criteria? Does it fit?

It does – so what we have here is strange language in a very familiar form. Have children had dreams like this, in which things are familiar and weird at the same time?

Read 'Mountain Lion' (pages 60–2) and 'Dingo Dingo' (pages 67–8), two poems on similar subjects. 'Mountain Lion' takes us well away from regular forms like the ballad, and all the way to Mexico. Write on a flip chart or board the meanings of the Spanish words: *Lobo* (wolf); *Qué tiene, amigo?* (What have you got there, my friend?); *León* (lion); *Hermoso es*! (It's beautiful!); *Sangre de Cristo*: Blood of Christ).

This poem is a kind of *elegy*, usually a poem commemorating someone who has died; here, an animal. What is the feeling in this poem? Is it anger directed at the hunters? No: it is sorrow, the sense of something lost. Which words towards the end of the poem make this clear? *(Yet what a gap in the world...)*

What can the children say about the way colour and light and dark are used in the poem? (It is a world which is cold and dark: the trees are *dark*, there is the *dark* and *gloom* of the valley, the desert is *dim*, the hunter is *dark-faced*; the colours are white, blue and green.) Compare these words and colours with those describing the lion and her lair, which are to do with light and warmth. Is it perhaps because the lion has been killed that the world is cold and dark? Is the lion a *symbol* of some sort?

101

SCHOLASTIC LITERACY CENTRES

CONT. . .

purple/blue

Poetry

CONT. . .

A glance tells us that this poem has no regular shape and therefore no regular rhythm; do the children know that this is *free verse*? Instead of stanzas, what does DH Lawrence use to give his poem shape? (Repetition of words and phrases; ask the children to find examples. Focus on the lines from *He trapped her...* to *...Beautiful dead eyes*.)

How is 'Dingo Dingo' similar to 'Mountain Lion'? In what ways is it different? Why isn't this free verse? (Because it is in regular stanzas with a consistent rhythm, even though it doesn't rhyme.) Lawrence's poem was very much about his *feelings* towards the lion; is this poem about Davis's feelings for the dingo? It isn't, but who do we have most sympathy with – at

first, anyway? Why is the dingo hunting? What is the 'twist' in the last stanza? We learn that the man is a professional hunter, paid to shoot dingoes, and he's hunting for the same reason as the dingo was: to provide for his family. Why does Davis use the phrase *his young*, rather than *his children*? Can the group work out that the poem is about the similarity between the man and the dingo – and why there are two *dingos* in the title?

Ask the children to read 'On the Antrim Coast' (pages 160–1) before the next session. Can they say why it is closer in form and feeling to 'Mountain Lion' than to 'Dingo Dingo'?

Read 'The Shoemakker' (page 81). This dialect poem is a wonderful rant; read it aloud with as much spite, and the best North Country accent, as you can muster. There's a powerful voice here; what words can the children offer to describe it? How would they picture the speaker?

Discuss the way the *sound* of the poem is vital. How do the rhythms work, and how do they change? Each stanza of this poem is really two parts,

with the last four lines as a varying refrain. (It could be set out in six stanzas, and sometimes is.) In these refrains the rhythm is strong and insistent; you can almost hear the shoemaker's wife clouting him over the head with one of his clogs as she spits out the words. Is there the same sort of rhythm in the first four lines of each part? This poem is anonymous; what does that suggest? (That it's very old, and that it was written down long after it was made up.)

How does the language depart from standard English? Would the poem be improved if it were written and punctuated 'properly'? Would that same voice still speak to us across the centuries?

This is one of just ten or so poems in the collection which have an identifiable narrator. You may already have read 'Overheard in County Sligo'; ask the children what connects the two. (A discontented wife.) But how are the two women narrators very different in personality and voice? What is the difference in their attitudes towards their situations? How does the form and sound of each one suit the narrator?

Ask the children to read 'Bess My Badger' (pages 146–8), and to think about who the narrator is, what he wants for Bess, and how his feelings about her change through the poem.

ACTIVITY NOTES

Reading aloud and performing poems

Objectives: to read poems aloud, individually and chorally, showing an awareness of rhythm, rhyme and other linguistic devices, and an ability to vary voice and expression appropriately; to enact poems.

Resources: copies of *The Forsaken Merman: The Wayland Book of Story Poems*.

Activity: Choose a selection of poems from the book for children to read aloud, as an ongoing activity. Encourage them to be intrepid when they read aloud. Try to cultivate a classroom culture in which children feel able to give, and take, advice and helpful criticism of each other's readings, and to co-operate in trying to achieve the best reading they can manage. Children should become increasingly able to respond to 'signals' in the poems which suggest tone, emphasis and pace.

Performance reading is an excellent tool for achieving understanding of a text as well as polishing delivery. Several poems in Doherty's collection have 'speaking parts' as well as a narrator. These include 'Robin Hood and Alan a Dale' (pages 37–41), Edward Lear's 'The Owl and the Pussy-Cat' (pages 49–51), 'The Wizard of Alderley Edge' (pages 73–4), Roald Dahl's 'Jack and the Beanstalk' (pages 100–4) and Charles Causley's 'By St Thomas Water' (pages 170–2). Some of the poems in the anthology are rather long. Discuss with the class how these long poems might be best divided into parts for group reading, and rehearse readings to ensure that the overall sense doesn't get lost.

Some poems may be turned into improvised or scripted playlets; others offer opportunities for 'mini-dramas' or short episodes of acting-out. Such poems include Matthew Sweeney's 'The Burglar' (page 36), Michael Rosen's 'Mart' (pages 52–5), Anne Born's 'Kopakona – Seal-Woman' (pages 91–4), Wilfrid Gibson's 'Flannan Isle' (pages 140–4). (See also the activity 'The eating of Albert Ramsbottom' below.)

A narrative poem log

Objective: to record and classify poems, as they are read.

Resources: photocopiable page 110, copies of *The Forsaken Merman: The Wayland Book of Story Poems*, writing materials.

Activity: In her foreword, Berlie Doherty suggests (rather poetically) some of the kinds of story to be found in her anthology. The photocopiable sheet offers a number of categories, in columns, which roughly correspond to and expand her list of story types, with additional columns for author, dialect and so on. The children should use it as a 'reading record' and also, by marking the relevant columns, to identify some of the characteristics of each poem. The author column will frequently feature *anon*. The title poem has been recorded, by way of example.

The eating of Albert Ramsbottom

Objective: to prepare for a performance reading of a poem.

Resources: photocopiable page 111, copies of *The Forsaken Merman: The Wayland Book of Story Poems*, props (see below), writing materials.

Activity: Ask a group of children to consider how they would organise a performance reading of 'The Lion and Albert' (pages 14–17). Use the photocopiable sheet to initiate discussion and record outcomes. When it comes to props, children may be ambitious but the only indispensable ones are those mentioned in the text: a stick with a horse's head handle, a cap and a purse. It would be excellent if you could contrive to have these available.

It would be useful to point out that *character* is depicted by speech, not description; what can the children deduce about the personalities of the speakers from what they say and how they say it?

Extension: Ask the group to perform the poem for the rest of the class, and review it.

Mart's version

Objective: to write an imaginative response to a poem based on close reading.
Resources: copies of *The Forsaken Merman: The Wayland Book of Story Poems*, paper, writing materials.
Activity: Ask the children to read 'Mart' (pages 52–5). Point out that although Michael Rosen doesn't use regular rhythm or rhyme (this is free verse), he is very thoughtful in the way he breaks up his story into lines. There is usually just one piece of information or one action in each line, for example:

The bus stopped.
I got on
Mart got on
The bus moved off.

Rosen also uses dialogue a good deal; that way, he gets little rhythmic sequences into the poem (...*he says*; *and Mum's going to say...*; *and if I say...* and so on).

Ask the children – working individually – to write the story of Michael's hat from Mart's point of view, trying to use a similar style to the original. They might need to consider these questions: why does Mart chuck the hat over the wall? Does he get the reaction he expects? What is Mart feeling as the bus approaches? What does he repeat, and why? Why does he dash off the bus early? Why doesn't he say anything or come in when he brings the hat back?

The wizard's transport café

Objective: to write a parody, using the structure of the ballad stanza.
Resources: copies of *The Forsaken Merman: The Wayland Book of Story Poems*, paper, writing materials.
Activity: Read at least the first two stanzas and the chorus of 'The Wizard of Alderley Edge' (pages 73–4), emphasising the rhythm, then ask the children to read the rest of the poem.

Challenge the children, working individually or in pairs, to write a parody of the poem. A possible first stanza could be:

From Bradford on a bright morning,
In a clapped-out Transit van,
A builder set out for Macclesfield
With his mate whose name was Dan.

The children may not be inspired by this opening; if so, let them invent their own. Remind them that the chorus occurs after *two* stanzas, and that they can vary it slightly if they wish. For the purposes of this activity, a story that 'makes sense' is less important than mastering the form; the children should be as nonsensically comical as they please.

Extension: Writing parodies is an excellent way of learning to master form. Encourage the children to write parodies of poems in this collection which have very regular forms, such as 'The Listeners' by Walter de la Mare (pages 33–5). For example:

> *'Is someone in there?' said the Teacher,*
> *Knocking on the toilet door...*

Or 'The Dying Cowboy' (pages 154–5):

> *As I snuck past the Headteacher's doorway,*
> *As I rolled up late for school yesterday...*

Three of a kind

Objectives: to note similarities and differences in poems with the same form; to express differences in mood and pace.

Resources: photocopiable page 112 (enlarged to A3 size, if necessary), copies of *The Forsaken Merman: The Wayland Book of Story Poems*, writing materials.

Activity: Explain that this activity involves comparing three poems by answering the questions on the photocopiable sheet. The children should work independently. Ask them to read (or re-read) Gillian Clarke's 'Overheard in County Sligo' (page 44), Lewis Carroll's 'Jabberwocky' (pages 63–4) and 'Ballad of the Drover' (pages 116–19). Taken as a group, these three poems should show how poems that are similar in form can differ dramatically in mood and purpose.

The children should write on the grid in note form rather than complete sentences. They should be able to use some technical terms, for example *rhyme scheme*. When writing about pace, they should be able to describe a rhythm and the way punctuation slows or quickens it, and to identify when the pace changes. For example, they might note that the rhythm gets faster in stanza 7 of 'Ballad of the Drover' and that this relates to an event in the poem (the drover tries to cross the river). Encourage the children to search for good words to describe mood – *regretful* is better than *sad*, for instance.

Verminous vocabulary

Objectives: to read a challenging poem closely; to deduce the meanings of words from their contexts; to check deductions using dictionaries; to compile a glossary.

Resources: photocopiable page 113, copies of *The Forsaken Merman: The Wayland Book of Story Poems*, good dictionaries, writing materials.

Activity: Ask the children to read the extract from Robert Browning's 'The Pied Piper of Hamelin' (pages 129–38). (As it is a lengthy poem, you may wish to suggest that they read it for homework before the activity.) Explain that they are going to attempt to define the more difficult words with which they may not be familiar. Remind them

SCHOLASTIC LITERACY CENTRES

that they will need to deduce meanings from the context. The photocopiable sheet lists a number of words from the first part of the poem. The children should complete the *My guess* lines before checking dictionary definitions. Encourage them to continue the formula, selecting further words from the poem to add to the 'Pied Piper' glossary and writing on the back of the sheet.

Extension: Browning's poem begs to be read aloud. You should try to bring out its pace and rhythms by reading at least one or two passages. The first 20 lines (down to *...sharps and flats*) contain a lovely change of pace. Ask the children to listen to the rat-charming passage (page 132, from *Into the street...* to *...plunged and perished!*) and then the exodus of Hamelin's children (pages 135–6, from *Once more he stept...* to *...sons and daughters!* page 136). Can they hear the similarities? Can they suggest why Browning wanted both these passages to sound like a hypnotic chant? How does a good reading-aloud of the poem help them to understand individual words?

Shock! Horror!

Objective: to retell the story of the Pied Piper in the form of a newspaper report.
Resources: copies of *The Forsaken Merman: The Wayland Book of Story Poems*, A3 paper, writing and drawing materials, a variety of newspapers.
Activity: Display the newspapers you have brought to the class and discuss the format and style of them. For example, do they all have a main picture on the front page? Does the front page have one main headline or several? Do some headlines leave out 'unnecessary' words, such as *the* or *an*? How do newspapers try to make stories seem exciting?

Tell the children that they are going to compile their own newspaper report on what happened in the town of Hamelin. (Children may work in pairs or in groups; you may want to allocate different parts of the poem for groups to summarise as a newspaper paragraph.) Suggest that the report (for *The Brunswick Bugle* or *The Hamelin Echo*, for example) should include some or all of the following: an attention-grabbing headline; a crisp summary of the events in Hamelin; quotes from the Mayor, distraught parents, the surviving child; 'photographs' (for example, of the Mayor and the empty playground of Hamelin Primary School); an artist's impression of the Pied Piper; comments from a Brunswick Police spokesperson.

The untold story

Objectives: to explore the situation in a poem; to write a version of it in prose or verse.
Resources: photocopiable page 114, copies of *The Forsaken Merman: The Wayland Book of Story Poems*, writing materials.
Activity: Read with the group Anne Stevenson's 'Utah' (page 145). Ask the children why this poem seems the odd one out in this collection. There's a story here, certainly, but the poet doesn't tell us it. The poem is like a photograph, or something glimpsed from a car, inviting us to imagine what happened just before and after it was taken. The photocopiable sheet poses questions to encourage conjecture. The children should arrive at answers, and then write the story behind the poem. They could do this either as a short prose piece or as a poem.

The dismal Dong

Objectives: to base original writing on a poem, maintaining its manner; to read closely and retell part of a poem.
Resources: photocopiable page 115, copies of *The Forsaken Merman: The Wayland Book of Story Poems*, writing and art materials.
Activity: Ask the children to read 'The Dong with a Luminous Nose' (pages 165–9), a tragic tale of thwarted love. If the group is working with you or an adult helper, some discussion of the poem would be useful; children may need help with a few difficult words such as *lurid* or *circlets*.

Provide the children with copies of the photocopiable sheet and ask them to write the message in the bottle, working individually. Encourage them to use words that rhyme; nonsense words should be permitted. The children should write the second response as either a) a recount of what the Dong did, or, better, b) a sequence of numbered instructions.
Extension: If the children haven't already done so, they should read 'The Jumblies' (pages 60–5 in *The Walker Book of Classic Poetry and Poets*). Which bits of text occur in both poems? How do the two poems fit into a time sequence?

A sting in the tale

Objective: to retell a traditional story in the manner of a poem from the anthology.
Resources: copies of *The Forsaken Merman: The Wayland Book of Story Poems*, paper, writing materials.
Activity: Alert readers might spot that four poems in the anthology are, in different ways, retellings of traditional, or 'fairy', tales. Ask the children if they can distinguish between the ways these poems relate to the original versions. Matilda Webb's 'The Homecoming' (pages 89–90) is an imaginative retelling of a small part of the Snow White story; Roald Dahl's 'Jack and the Beanstalk' (pages 100–4) is a comic version which takes liberties with the traditional tale, updating the setting and using slang; LJ Anderson's 'Beauty and the Beast' (pages 156–7) is an emotive and atmospheric summary of the story as told by the Beast; and Wilma Horsburgh's 'The Train to Glasgow' (pages 76–8) is a cumulative verse parody of 'The House That Jack Built'.

With the group, compile a list of traditional tales with a view to writing verse retellings. 'The Three Little Pigs' suggests its own three-part structure (and *straw*, *sticks* and *brick* are easy words to rhyme). 'Little Red Riding Hood', told (with bloodthirsty relish) from the Wolf's point of view could be interesting. In the first instance, children should attempt their writing individually; at a later stage, if there are poems which seem promising and in need of some polishing, they can collaborate.

I would have chosen these

Objective: to make and justify a choice of poems for inclusion in an anthology.
Resources: copies of *The Forsaken Merman: The Wayland Book of Story Poems* and *The Walker Book of Classic Poetry and Poets*, paper, writing materials.
Activity: Ask the children to identify narrative poems in *The Walker Book of Classic Poetry and Poets* which Berlie Doherty has *not* included in *The Forsaken Merman: The Wayland Book of Story Poems*. These are Lord Byron's 'The Destruction of Sennacherib'

(pages 27–9), Henry Wadsworth Longfellow's 'Paul Revere's Ride' (pages 46–51), Edward Lear's 'The Jumblies' (pages 60–5), Robert Browning's 'My Last Duchess' (pages 66–9), Banjo Paterson's 'Waltzing Matilda' (pages 104–6) and 'Mulga Bill's Bicycle' (pages 107–9), and TS Eliot's 'Journey of the Magi' (pages 144–5).

Ask the children to explain in writing which of these poems they would have included if they were the editor, and why.

Alternatively, ask them to identify poets which appear in both collections but are represented by different poems. (These are Tennyson, Lear, Judith Wright, Longfellow, Emily Dickinson, WB Yeats, Paterson and Browning.) Do they prefer the selection in one book to that in the other? Why? Are there poems by the same poet that Doherty should have included? (Children might think, for example, that Lear's 'The Jumblies' should be in there because it 'goes with' 'The Dong with a Luminous Nose'; or that Banjo Paterson's 'Mulga Bill's Bicycle' should be alongside 'The Man from Snowy River' to show that he can be a comic poet, too.)

Words to wonder at

Objectives: to understand the concept of dialect verse; to read dialect verse and deduce the meanings of unfamiliar words from their contexts.
Resources: photocopiable page 116, copies of *The Forsaken Merman: The Wayland Book of Story Poems*, writing materials, good dictionaries.
Activity: Explain (or remind the children of) the difference between *accent* (the way that the pronunciation of standard English varies from person to person and from place to place) and *dialect* (the use of words and sentence structures unique to a particular area). Ask the children if they can identify poems in the anthology that use dialect. There's a difference between true dialect words such as *silkie* and *ken* in 'The Silkie of Sule Skerry' (pages 42–3) or *ferlie* in 'Thomas Rymer' (pages 162–4), and archaic words such as *quoth* and *wilt* – which were once commonly used verbs – in 'Robin Hood and Alan a Dale' (pages 37–41).

The photocopiable sheet offers a grid on which children can record dialect words from any poem and then deduce and check their meanings (you may need to guide them through an appropriate dictionary either in print or on screen). Guessing the correct meanings would be a bonus; but the criterion should be that the children offer definitions which make plausible sense within the context.
Extension: You may be fortunate enough to live in an area where dialect survives; if so, challenge children to compile a 'dialect dictionary'. Older relatives might be a good source, and local librarians or museum staff might be able to help. In many areas, libraries keep books of local language and folklore. These are sometimes a good springboard for children's writing.

The voice from under the ground

Objective: to demonstrate understanding of a narrative poem by retelling it in prose.
Resources: copies of *The Forsaken Merman: The Wayland Book of Story Poems*, paper, writing materials.
Activity: Read Charles Causley's 'By St Thomas Water' (pages 170–2) to the children. This magical poem recalls a childhood experience. It centres on a simple joke – children taking literally a tombstone inscription, *'He is not dead but sleeping'*, and

scaring themselves witless. Causley's figurative language is wonderfully rich – the sun crawling *like a crab* across *the beach of sky*, for example – but the narrative is essentially simple.

Ask the children to retell the story in prose. They should write it in the first person, as the boy in the poem, and take the story up to and including the penultimate stanza. Encourage the children to include descriptive writing, taking their cues from Causley's verse, for example the voice *as clear as blood*, the lettering as *black as coffin-lead*.

Extension: Discuss the final stanza with the children. Do they grasp the idea that the narrator is now old, nearer death himself? Why, then, would he be more interested in knowing what the grave has to tell him; why, now, is he more willing to listen?

The sea caves

Objective: to annotate a verse extract, marking 'textual events' and particular techniques.

Resources: photocopiable page 117, copies of *The Forsaken Merman: The Wayland Book of Story Poems*, writing and colouring materials.

Activity: The photocopiable sheet provides an extract from the title poem (the passage is on page 10). It is not absolutely necessary to read the whole poem, but it would be helpful. Explain, if you need to, what annotation is. Ask the children to mark (using colours, if they wish) the features of the verse that they notice and recognise (as shown). They should write any thoughts or questions on the paper in note form (as shown) which might help them to talk or write about the poem. A list of terms they might find useful is at the foot of the sheet.

Extension: Ask the children to turn their notes into continuous prose.

109

SCHOLASTIC LITERACY CENTRES

Name

Date

A narrative poem log

Title of poem	page no.	heroic	comic	tragic	fantastical	mysterious	legendary	dialect	Standard English	Author
The Forsaken Merman	9			✓	✓	✓			✓	Matthew Arnold

Name _____ Date _____

The eating of Albert Ramsbottom

Use this sheet to help you prepare for a performance of 'The Lion and Albert'.

❏ How many **characters** appear?

❏ How many **readers** do we need?

The **narrator** has a big part: shall we share it between two people? How?

The **cast** (who plays the parts):

How many locations are there? How do we show changes of place?

Do we see the Ramsbottoms walking about in the first part of the poem or do they walk on at stanza 4?

Do we show the lion? If so, how? Or do we use sound effects somehow?

What props do we need? What things are in the text that we need to have?

Illustration © 1998 Nick Maland

purple/blue

Poetry

photocopiable

SCHOLASTIC

Name   Date

Three of a kind

Read the three poems named along the top of this grid, then see if you can answer the questions by writing in the appropriate boxes.

	'Overheard in County Sligo' (page 44)	'Jabberwocky' (pages 63 to 64)	'Ballad of the Drover' (pages 116 to 119)
Subject What is the poem about?			
Narrator Is there a narrator? First person or third person?			
Form Is the poem written in the normal ballad stanza? If not, how is it different?			
Pace How would you describe the rhythm of the poem?			
Mood What is the mood or atmosphere of the poem like? Pick out key words which express it.			

SCHOLASTIC

purple/blue

Poetry

SCHOLASTIC LITERACY CENTRES

Name

Date

Verminous vocabulary

'The Pied Piper of Hamelin' has quite a lot of strange words in it. Here is
the beginning of a list of some of them. Try to guess the meaning of each
one by reading the poem carefully for clues. Then look up the definition in a
dictionary. (You might need to use a really big one!) How close were your
guesses? Add more words, guesses and definitions as you read through the
poem, continuing on the back of this sheet.

pied

My guess: _____

Definition: _____

ditty

My guess: _____

Definition: _____

vermin

My guess: _____

Definition: _____

noddy

My guess: _____

Definition: _____

ermine

My guess: _____

Definition: _____

determine

My guess: _____

Definition: _____

consternation

My guess: _____

Definition: _____

mutinous

My guess: _____

Definition: _____

glutinous

My guess: _____

Definition: _____

Name _____ Date _____

The untold story

Read 'Utah' by Anne Stevenson (page 145). It's very mysterious, like a photograph without a caption. What's the story? Try thinking up answers to the questions on this page.

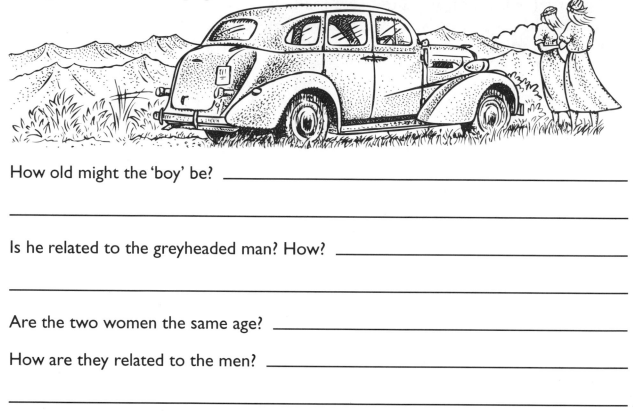

How old might the 'boy' be? _____

_____

Is he related to the greyheaded man? How? _____

_____

Are the two women the same age? _____

How are they related to the men? _____

_____

What's the weather like? _____

_____

What's dead in the dust? Has the 'boy' shot it? Why? _____

_____

_____

Why is the 'boy' crying? _____

_____

What is the greyheaded man saying? _____

_____

_____

✹ SCHOLASTIC

Name   Date

The dismal Dong

It's tragic, really, what happens to the Dong – driven quite mad by losing his Jumbly girl. One thing he might have tried is sending her a message in a bottle. Here's the bottle: write the message. Is it in prose or verse? Is it sense or nonsense?

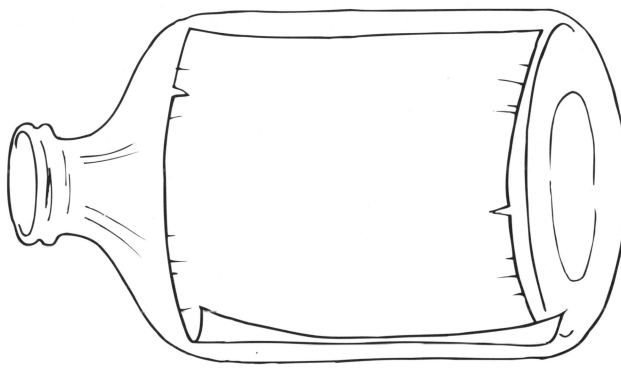

How do you make a Dong's luminous Nose? **Either** explain how the Dong did it; **or** write a set of instructions. Then, on the back of this sheet, draw, colour and label the Nose.

purple/blue

Poetry

photocopiable

SCHOLASTIC

Name

Date

Words to wonder at

Title of poem:

Country or place of origin:

Non-standard English and dialect words	Meanings guessed from context	Definitions

Words we need to research:

purple/blue

Poetry

Name   Date

The sea caves

This is an extract from the title poem of Berlie Doherty's anthology. Mark
on this sheet things you notice, such as those listed at the foot of the page.
Underline, link words together, write little comments in the margin, as
shown. Use different-coloured pens if it helps.

it's the Merman's voice. He tells the story.

repetition

Children dear, was it yesterday
We heard the sweet bells over the bay?
In the caverns where we lay,
Through the surf and through the swell,
The far-off sound of a silver bell?

alliteration. Lots of s's everywhere! Why?

Sand-strewn caverns, cool and deep,

Where the winds are all asleep;

Where the spent lights quiver and gleam,

Where the salt weed sways in the stream,

Where the sea-beasts, ranged all round,

Feed in the ooze of their pasture-ground;

Where the sea-snakes coil and twine,

Dry their mail and bask in the brine;

Where great whales come sailing by,

Sail and sail, with unshut eye,

Round the world for ever and aye?

When did music come this way?

Children dear, was it yesterday?

repetition	the same word or sound appearing more than once
rhythm	a pattern of beats running through the poem
alliteration	words close together which begin with the same sound
couplet	two consecutive lines which rhyme
end-stopped	lines which end with a punctuation mark
assonance	vowel sounds which echo each other, such as b<u>ea</u>ch, h<u>ea</u>t
consonance	consonant sounds which echo each other, such as bi<u>tt</u>er, pa<u>tt</u>er

purple/blue
Poetry

117

SCHOLASTIC LITERACY CENTRES

photocopiable
■SCHOLASTIC

118

Shocks, scandals and gruesome murders

Background

This text traces the connections between ancient songs and stories (the oral tradition which Berlie Doherty refers to in her introduction to *The Forsaken Merman: The Wayland Book of Story Poems*) and today's tabloid newspapers and advertising. What's really interesting about that connection is that the street balladeers used poetic techniques – rhythm, rhyme and music – to communicate with people who couldn't read very well, if at all; and that some of these techniques are still being used. (Headline writers still love rhyme and alliteration, for example.) It should be useful – and fun – to explore and experiment with the connections between narrative poems, ballads and newspaper reporting and to think about the different ways they tell a 'story'.

■ Read the text on photocopiable page 120 and refer the children to Berlie Doherty's foreword to *The Forsaken Merman: The Wayland Book of Story Poems*. Ask them if they can make the connection between the two texts; can they use the phrase *the oral tradition* with confidence? Which part of the extra text connects with Doherty's comment about *village gatherings*? (The last three sentences.) Can they grasp that even in an age when printing was cheap, the oral tradition was still vital because illiteracy continued to be commonplace? Would they agree, from their reading of Doherty's anthology, that the things listed in the first sentence of 'Shocks, scandals and gruesome murders' could well be subjects of narrative poems? Can they suggest a poem from *The Forsaken Merman: The Wayland Book of Story Poems* which fits something in that list? (For example, *shipwreck* – 'The Wreck of the Hesperus' or 'Sir Patrick Spens'. There's plenty of choice for 'tragic death'!)

■ Swift's narrative poem on photocopiable page 121 clearly echoes the extra text. It's a bit challenging, but the gist should be clear enough. (You should perhaps explain that when Clinch urges his 'Comrades' to *Nor slip this Occasion to follow your Trade* he is urging his fellow thieves not to miss the chance of picking a few pockets in the crowd.) Can the children hear the jog-along rhythm in Swift's lines? Is this a conventional ballad? No, but it deliberately echoes the rhythms and simple rhymes of 'hanging ballads'. There are some cruel ironies here: ask the children to question the words *clever* and *Hero*. But who's worse: the criminal or the sightseers? Suggest that the children decide, before they begin writing, what *kind* of account they intend to write: an eyewitness, first-person account? A news-style report? A piece that could be part of a made-up story?

■ The extra text suggests a similarity between ballad 'hacks' and modern tabloid journalists. Photocopiable page 122 challenges children to be such journalists and invent sensational headlines and sub-heads to poems in *The Forsaken Merman: The Wayland Book of Story Poems*. Suggest that they lift lines or events from their chosen poems for their sub-heads, as in the example. Can they identify the poem on which it is based? ('Jabberwocky', pages 63–4.)

■ Explain to the children that because the kind of street ballads described in 'Shocks, scandals and gruesome murders' were cheap and disposable, many have been destroyed over the years. People didn't value them or preserve them. There must be thousands of lost stories which were never printed, which never survived the oral tradition. Photocopiable page 123 offers children an opportunity for a bit of creative silliness by asking them to restore a verse or two of a 'lost' ballad. Remind them that, as Berlie Doherty and the extra text suggest, they will be writing sensational journalism before there were sensational newspapers. You might also suggest that the time traveller is a schoolchild from the 21st century.

__ assessment

ASSESSMENT NOTES

What's the story?

Assessment focus: to recognise the story elements of narrative poems when presented in a different form.

Resources: photocopiable page 124, copies of *The Forsaken Merman: The Wayland Book of Story Poems*, writing materials.

Activity: 'What's the story?' consists of brief 'newspaper cuttings'. Each one should suggest the storyline from a poem in the anthology. Working alone, children should try to work out which poems are being alluded to and record the title and page number.

The answers are: 1. 'The Wreck of the Hesperus', page 69; 2. 'Ballad of the Drover', page 116; 3. 'Robin Hood and Alan a Dale', page 37; 4. 'The Lion and Albert', page 14; 5. 'Jack and the Beanstalk', page 100; 6. 'The Dong with a Luminous Nose', page 165.

Nightmare at sea

Assessment focus: to apply understanding of narrative verse and some of the techniques of poetry to a previously unseen poem; to make conjectures about the story.

Resources: photocopiable page 125, writing materials.

Activity: The photocopiable sheet provides a short extract from Coleridge's 'The Rime of the Ancient Mariner'. It's from Part II of the poem; the Ancient Mariner has shot the albatross which has been following the ship, bringing good luck. Now the ship is becalmed and the crew is dying of thirst.

Good answers to question 1 will mention *ballad* and/or *ballad stanza*. Good answers to question 2 might mention regular stanzas; the same rhyme scheme in the first two stanzas, with an extra rhyme in the third; lots of repetition (of words, of phrases, of whole lines); alliteration (for example, *drop... drink*); the slow, heavy rhythm. In answering question 3, the children should be able to suggest that all that repetition and the slow, plodding beat convey the scary sense of stillness, of being *stuck* (a key word), of being baked alive and unable to move. You can almost hear the storyteller, the narrator, going mad with thirst in the third stanza. In answering question 4, children should give free rein to their imagination, while responding to the words *nightmarish sea voyage* in the rubric.

Shocks, scandals and gruesome murders

A terrible shipwreck, a highway robbery, a Royal scandal, a brutal murder, a public hanging, a tragic death. These were the subjects of the best-selling poems 200 years ago. Who wrote them? Lord Byron? William Wordsworth? No, they were written by anonymous 'hacks' who churned out 'street ballads' that were cheaply printed and illustrated and sold in the streets of London and other major cities. They were often composed to be sung to popular tunes, which made them easier to remember and enabled the street-sellers, or 'hawkers', to sing them.

In an age when few people could read, before there were mass-circulation newspapers, these crude narrative poems were how most people heard stories and got the news – and, just like today, the more shocking, violent and rude it was, the better it sold. (That's one of the reasons why the authors of these ballads remained anonymous – they were such liars!)

'Hanging ballads' were especially popular. In the days before a public hanging was due to take place, the hacks would be very busy, composing ballads to be sold to the excited crowd. These ballads often contained a lurid account of the murder (about which the writer knew little, of course), a description of the murderer (whom the writer had never seen) and the murderer's last words spoken from the scaffold (which hadn't been spoken yet). Often, ballad-writers would reuse an execution speech made by an earlier murderer, or use a standardised plea for forgiveness, changing just a few details. No one seemed to mind too much.

Perhaps someone who could read would travel to the nearest city to watch a hanging and buy a ballad as a souvenir. When he got home, he would read it to his friends and neighbours. That's how poetry spread the news, 250 years ago.

Name   Date

Clever Tom Clinch
going to be Hanged (1726)

As clever Tom Clinch, while the rabble was bawling,
Rode stately through Holburn, to die in his calling;
He stopt at the George for a bottle of sack,
And promis'd to pay for it when he'd come back.
His Waistcoat and Stockings, and Breeches were white,
His cap had a new Cherry Ribbon to ty't.
The Maids to the Doors and the Balconies ran,
And said, Lack-a-day! He's a proper young Man.
But, as from the Windows the Ladies he spy'd,
Like a Beau in the Box, he bow'd low on each side;
And when his last Speech the loud Hawkers did cry,
He swore from his Cart, it was all a damn'd Lye.
The Hangman for Pardon fell down on his Knee;
Tom gave him a Kick in the Guts for his Fee.
Then said, I must speak to the People a little,
But I'll see you all damn'd before I will whittle.
My honest Friend Wild, may he long hold his Place,
He lengthen'd my Life with a whole Year of Grace.
Take courage, dear Comrades, and be not afraid,
Nor slip this Occasion to follow your Trade.
My Conscience is clear, and my Spirits are calm,
And thus off I go without Pray'r-Book or Psalm.
Then follow the Patience of clever *Tom Clinch*,
Who hung like a Hero, and never would flinch.

Jonathan Swift

GLOSSARY

calling work, profession   **Beau in the Box** wealthy young man at the theatre
sack wine   **Wild** Jonathan Wild, an infamous highway robber
whittle beg forgiveness   **slip** lose

---

1. Write an account of what happens in this poem, using the information in 'Shocks, scandals and gruesome murders'.

2. What might have been in Clinch's last speech that the hawkers were selling?

3. Is Jonathan Swift really saying what he means in this poem? What do you think he felt about:

❑ Tom Clinch   ❑ the spectators?

Name _____ Date _____

Here is the news

Which poem in *The Forsaken Merman: The Wayland Book of Story Poems* might fit this screaming headline?

BEAMISH BOY BEHEADS BLOOD-CRAZED BEAST
'FRABJOUS DAY,' SAYS FATHER

poem _____ page _____

Now make up sensational headlines for these poems from *The Forsaken Merman: The Wayland Book of Story Poems*:

❏ 'Little Billee' (pages 96 to 97)

❏ 'The Dying Cowboy' (pages 154 to 155)

❏ 'The Wreck of the Hesperus' (pages 69 to 72)

❏ 'The Burglar' (page 36)

❏ 'Miss Peacock' (page 75)

Name   Date

A lost ballad

On the 1st of April 1743 a time machine appeared close to a remote village in southern England. The only witness to its appearance was an anonymous hack who quickly dashed off a ballad about the events that followed. Unfortunately, almost all of the ballad has been lost. Only a handful of stanzas survive, and two of them are printed below. Can you add one or two more? And what might the title of the ballad be?

Title: _____

'Twas while I was wand'ring in Witless Wood
That the THING appeared to me;
And I'll never forget that April Day
In Seventeen Forty-Three.

A great big shiny Box it was,
The size of a Horse and Cart;
It appeared with a Flash and mighty Crash
That almost stopped my Heart.

_____

_____

_____

_____

_____

_____

_____

_____

Name _____   Date _____

What's the story?

These 'clippings' suggest how newspapers might have reported some of the stories in *The Forsaken Merman: The Wayland Book of Story Poems*. Can you work out which poem each one refers to?

❶

NORMAN'S WOE CLAIMS NEW VICTIMS
Captain 'ignored warnings'. Corpse of girl found tied to mast.

Poem: _____

_____

_____

page: _____

❷

Rider and dog drown in flash-flood
Death of popular Queensland man – fiancée 'heart-broken'

Poem: _____ page: _____

❸

Following the raid on the church, the groom, Sir Percy Greyshanks, 74, was "deeply disappointed and upset" according to friends.

A spokesman for the Sheriff said, "We are seeking about 25 men. This was clearly a carefully planned and well-organised kidnap. As yet we have no news of the missing bride. We are asking the public to keep a special lookout for three men: a man with a harp, a very large man and a man wearing scarlet tights."

Poem: _____ page: _____

❹

"We're right baffled," said a zoo official. "Our Wallace has never done owt like that before. He's normally as placid as can be. We can only assume he must have been provoked in some way. His stomach is very upset, I can tell you that."

Poem: _____

_____

_____

page: _____

❺

BOY DENIES GIANT PLANT IS GENETICALLY MODIFIED

Poem: _____ page: _____

❻

Who glows there?

Several residents of the village of Lower Chankly have reported seeing an eerie light moving around the Gromboolian Plain each night this week. "It's usually around midnight," said Mrs Irene Lightfoot of Chankly Hall. "I wonder if it's one of those UFO things."

Colonel Oliver Sudden of Grombool Terrace scoffed at the idea. "Just some daft chap looking for his girlfriend, I shouldn't wonder," he said, tapping his nose mysteriously.

Poem: _____ page: _____

124

Name   Date

Nightmare at sea

This is a short extract from a long narrative poem about a nightmarish sea voyage. Read it carefully, listening to the sound it makes in your head, and then answer the questions. Write on the back of the sheet if you run out of room.

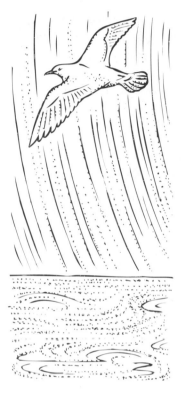

All in a hot and copper sky,
The bloody Sun, at noon,
Right up above the mast did stand,
No bigger than the Moon.

Day after day, day after day,
We stuck, nor breath nor motion;
As idle as a painted ship
Upon a painted ocean.

Water, water, everywhere,
And all the boards did shrink;
Water, water, everywhere,
Nor any drop to drink.

Samuel Taylor Coleridge

1. What sort of poem is this? What form is it written in?

_____

_____

2. Write three things you notice about the way language is patterned in this extract.

_____

_____

_____

3. What is the feeling in this piece? How do the pattern and sound of the language help to create this feeling?

_____

_____

_____

4. What's the story? What might have happened before this, and what might happen later?

_____

_____

Hello New!

Edited by John Agard

This is a rich collection of specially commissioned poems on the theme of 'newness', containing work by an almost shocking constellation of star writers: Roger McGough, Opal Palmer Adisa, Helen Dunmore, Ian McMillan, Brian Patten, Carol Ann Duffy, Geraldine McCaughrean, Grace Nichols, Wendy Cope; there are all these and many more in a handsome volume illustrated with frisky black-and-white drawings by Lydia Monks. Really, this book is a must for every school. In terms of level, all these poems are accessible to most children.

■ Begin (as the poets themselves must have done) by considering the possible meanings and connotations of the word *new*. Ask the children to offer synonyms, for example *novel, unspoilt, different, fresh, recent, latest, original*. What are the different connotations of *new* in *new shoes; new school; new baby*? Explore the connections between *new* and words like *hope, clean, innocent*.

■ Because this anthology is built around a single (if complex) idea, there are multiple routes through it; almost every poem has some connection with almost every other poem. John Agard has cleverly ordered the poems into connected mini-sequences; but, with the above ideas in mind, read three poems together: 'Smiles Like Roses' (pages 11–12), 'A New Blue Bike' (page 13) and 'First Lamb' (page 70). What connects them? It's the newness of the year, of spring: Helen Dunmore's poem blissfully greets the sun again; the tools that John Rice's children are using to mend their bike are *warming their winter metal*; Gillian Clarke celebrates the first new-born lamb of the year. But how different in form these three poems are! Discuss with the children the singing of Dunmore's poem, the business-like matter-of-factness of Rice's, the snugly organised rhyme of Clarke's poem, so full of sound and tastes and smells.

■ Newness can also be strangeness. Read 'New Boy' (pages 38–9). Finding oneself in a new place – a new school – can be traumatic. Ask the children what they think Peter Sansom's character is doing in this poem. (Is he preparing himself mentally in case he is bullied, acting out all the terrible things that he knows could be done to him; or is he really being bullied, but covering it up by pretending that it is being done by himself?) Do the children recognise these experiences? Has Sansom got them right? Has he missed any? Opal Palmer Adisa's 'Keeping my Own Company' (pages 42–3) looks at the strangeness of growing up, but what is the feeling in this poem? Can the children relate to both the sense of disturbance in the poem and the optimism which ends it?

■ There is one truly great poem in this anthology: 'Number One and the Butterfly' by Ursula Fanthorpe (pages 96–7). It deals with sibling rivalry, jealousy, and takes a dissenting swipe at newness. It's very subtle; its meaning is elusive. Share it with the children, and let it root.

Collected Poems for Children

Gareth Owen

A treasure house from one of the best children's poets, this is Gareth Owen's three collections of verse (*Salford Road*, *Song of the City* and *My Granny is a Sumo Wrestler*) in one volume. There's a strong autobiographical thread running throughout the book, but Owen usually looks at his childhood experiences through an older, somewhat ironic eye. This is a rich collection which should ring bells in any classroom (and adult memory).

■ If the children have read Peter Sansom's 'New Boy' from *Hello New!*, read Owen's poem on the same subject (page 172). How do they differ in point of view? How does Owen's use of the first person make his poem very different in attitude from Sansom's? (The speaker is talking about his own sense of shame that he didn't intervene in the bullying.) Can the children spot that Owen's poem is written in the form of a ballad?

■ Read and compare two more school-based poems: 'Friday Morning Last Two Lessons is Games Day' (pages 50–2) and 'Drama Lesson' (pages 65–6). Encourage the children to find things in the first poem which suggest a fairly distant past (despite being written in the present tense). How do their own games lessons differ from this? An idea which links the two poems is that school experiences which are comically inauthentic nevertheless fuel the child's imagination. Can the children express this in their own words?

■ In *Talking Turkeys* Benjamin Zephaniah uses all sorts of 'non-poetic' forms for his poetry. Read Owen's 'The Commentator' (pages 96–8), a wonderfully comic use of football commentary to evoke a back-yard kick-about which goes wrong. Who's 'speaking' this commentary? How does the triumphant tone of it differ sharply and ironically from the actual events? This is, incidentally, a delightfully innovative example of narrative verse.

■ Read the short sequence of poems which begins with 'Space Shot' (page 155) and ends with 'Shed in Space' (pages 161–2). Ask the group if they can identify the theme of these poems. More demandingly, ask the children if they can identify the differences. ('Space Shot' is a vivid description of a real event; 'Moonscape 2400', 'Lessons in History' and 'Message Understood' are 'science fiction' poems, each with a twist in the tail; 'Shed in Space' is a whimsical evocation of a family memory.)

■ Read and compare two poems on the same subject from the earliest and the latest poems: 'The Cat' (pages 20–1) and 'Rubble' (pages 226–8). Which is regular; which is free verse? What does the earlier poem try to do? (See the world from a cat's point of view.) How does this differ from Rubble? (Rubble is written from a human point of view, but ends up by imagining the cat's thoughts.) Which is funnier? Which is the more sophisticated?

Meeting Midnight

Carol Ann Duffy

Duffy's collection is challenging, sometimes even frightening; it is also rather brilliant. There's humour in the poems, but no 'light' verse. Duffy doesn't shirk from those lurking anxieties that most children – most people – often feel, but she has a marvellous ability to present them in vivid images. In the poem 'A Worry' (pages 50–1), a child wonders:

And what about other girls?
What about boys?
Do they have worry growing like fungi
over their books and toys?

■ Several poems in the collection are narratives, and would not be out of place in Berlie Doherty's *The Forsaken Merman: The Wayland Book of Story Poems*. Begin with 'Snowball' (pages 30–3). Discuss Duffy's lovely use of metaphor, for example *The cold squeezed like a bully's hug*, the sinister connection between *sprats* and *the white bite of the world*. How does the child feel at the end? Is the moon-sized snowball a *crime* or a beautiful achievement?

■ Next, read 'Queens' (pages 18–21) and then 'The Duke of Fire and the Duchess of Ice' (pages 34–5). Can the children identify the idea that links them? (The attraction of opposites.) In 'Queens', one queen is cold and thin, the other warm and fat. Ask the children if they can see how Duffy uses colour, clothes, food and pastimes, verbs and adjectives to build up this contrast. How does the thin queen feel at the end of the poem? How is colour used similarly in 'The Duke of Fire and the Duchess of Ice'? Even though the Duchess of Ice thought that *with one kiss she would melt*, she is not 'killed' by the Duke of Fire at the end of the poem; he brings her to life. Whereas ice is something which kills life, isn't rain something which gives life?

■ Sometimes Duffy tells a story by not telling it. Read 'Poker' (pages 16–17) and ask the children if they can work the story out. (A cheat gets shot and thrown from a ship for concealing a winning card up his sleeve.)

■ For a beautiful example of how a poem can be stitched together by a sequence of rhymes and half-rhymes, read 'Sharp Freckles' (page 43), in which a child describes her father. Look at the words at the ends of the lines, and the way they hold the poem together even though it has no particular rhythm.

■ Finally, look at Duffy's use of metaphor again. Read the first part of 'Boys' (pages 22–4), which is about St Paul's Cathedral. Metaphor can do such a lot of work with just a few words. What Duffy does here is use personification (contained in *I wake; gargle; shake; curls; thoughts*) to make us do the impossible: to imagine an ancient building as a person waking up. And what a brilliant feat, to bring the words *gargle* and *gargoyles* together within three lines to make both sense and rich metaphor!